ASPIRE

130

PROJECTS

TO GET YOU INTO

FILM
MAKING

ASPIRE

130 PROJECTS TO GET YOU INTO FILM MAKING

Elliot Grove

BARRON'S

A QUARTO BOOK

First edition for the United States, its territories and dependencies, and Canada published in 2009 by Barron's Educational Series, Inc.

All inquiries should be addressed to:
Barron's Educational Series, Inc.
250 Wireless Boulevard
Hauppauge, NY 11788
www.barronseduc.com

ISBN-13: 978-0-7641-4296-3
ISBN-10: 0-7641-4296-8

Library of Congress Control Number: 2009928377

QUAR.WOFS

Conceived, designed, and produced by:
Quarto Publishing plc
The Old Brewery
6 Blundell Street
London
N7 9BH

Script doctor: Sally Maceachern
Additional text: Grace Sargeant (makeup); Dan Martin (low-budget special effects); Kevin Lindenmuth (examples); Chris Patmore (rights)
Key grip: Xavier Rashid
"Best boys": Sarah Romeo; Grace Leong
Runner: Samantha Lucas
Art director: Caroline Guest
Art editor: Emma Clayton
Designer: Louise Clements
Design assistant: Saffron Stocker
Photographer: Simon Pask
Picture researcher: Sarah Bell
Creative director: Moira Clinch
Gaffer: Paul Carslake
Color separation in Singapore by PICA Digital Pte Ltd
Printed in Singapore by Star Standard Industries (PTE) Ltd

9 8 7 6 5 4 3 2 1

Contents

Chapter 1

Chapter 2

Chapter 3

Chapter 4

Foreword

There has never been a better time than now to break into the film industry.

Significant technological advances in recent years mean that filmmaking is now accessible to anyone with merely a few simple electronic tools at their disposal, such as a cell phone and a laptop. This same technology has revolutionized movie distribution so that films are now readily available to watch on the Internet and on cell phones.

This book takes you through all the steps you need to know in order to make your movie—starting with the idea you have in your head, through the principles of production, and, ultimately, how to get your film in front of an audience.

All movies start with an idea. My guess is that you already have an idea for a movie. In section one I guide you through the step-by-step process of getting that idea out of your head and onto paper—written in the language of film—that is, in the style and format that professional filmmakers understand.

Once you have the script, you still need to get your movie made somehow. Section two explains how to take some actors, a camera, and some lights, and start shooting your film in the most cost-effective and visually aesthetic way possible.

In sections three and four, you will find out how to promote and distribute your finished movie so that people all over the world have the chance to see it.

Elliot Grove (fourth from right) on the set of a 35 mm shoot.

Each section has a series of short and snappy exercises designed to get you up and running as soon as possible—writing, producing, and directing your own film.

For 20 years at London's Raindance Film Festival, I have met and worked with some incredibly talented filmmakers. Some, like Guy Ritchie and Matthew Vaughn, have found fame as well as fortune. Other very talented filmmakers with whom I have had the great privilege of working are still wrestling with the commercial aspects of the business.

In that time, I have learned many tricks of the trade, which I am now passing on. It is my hope that these lessons will be useful to you as you find out how to express your ideas cinematically and avoid some of the pitfalls along the way.

Happy filmmaking!

ELLIOT GROVE

6 Essentials to becoming a filmmaker

These are the basic requirements if you want to become a successful filmmaker. Success can be measured as fortune or fame—in other words, the money you earn or the number of people who see your film.

1 Script
How many times have you seen a movie and asked yourself: "How did they get the money for that?" Think back. Was it because the acting, editing, or camerawork was bad? Almost certainly the movie was terrible because the screenplay was bad.

Whether or not you write it yourself, your first task is to learn to identify the brilliant screenplay.

2 Funding
Once you have your screenplay, and before you do anything else, you will need to get ahold of some money. One of the purposes of this book is to show you how little money you might actually need to make a good movie.

3 Telephone
This is the most essential piece of equipment that you need to make a movie. To put it another way, you need to develop excellent interpersonal communication skills.

4 Savvy
You can't be taught good business sense, but you can pick up tips that will help you figure it out your own way.

5 Energy
You'll need heaps and heaps of it. When you are making a film, you will wake up each morning and complain that you have never felt so tired in your life. You'll need to find an inner source of energy that you never knew you possessed to help you power through.

6 Talent
This is important, but not essential. Talent is described in the industry as the ability to make a movie that is successful well within the scope and limitations of the budget.

The film crew

Creating a film requires a whole army of people with many varied skills. Here are the people you will find on a professional shoot.

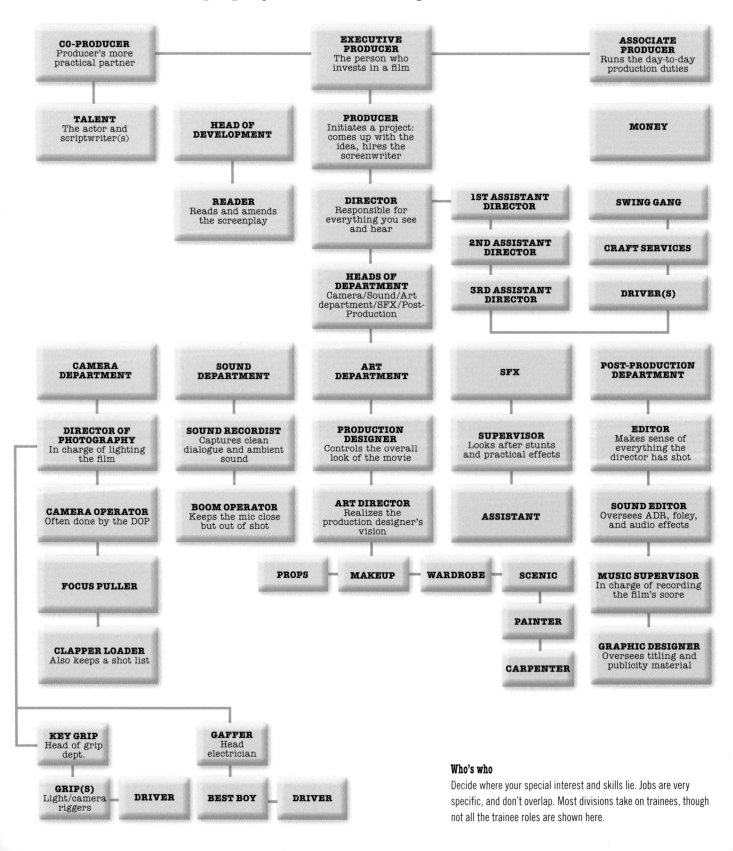

CO-PRODUCER
Producer's more practical partner

EXECUTIVE PRODUCER
The person who invests in a film

ASSOCIATE PRODUCER
Runs the day-to-day production duties

TALENT
The actor and scriptwriter(s)

HEAD OF DEVELOPMENT

PRODUCER
Initiates a project: comes up with the idea, hires the screenwriter

MONEY

READER
Reads and amends the screenplay

DIRECTOR
Responsible for everything you see and hear

1ST ASSISTANT DIRECTOR

SWING GANG

2ND ASSISTANT DIRECTOR

CRAFT SERVICES

HEADS OF DEPARTMENT
Camera/Sound/Art department/SFX/Post-Production

3RD ASSISTANT DIRECTOR

DRIVER(S)

CAMERA DEPARTMENT

SOUND DEPARTMENT

ART DEPARTMENT

SFX

POST-PRODUCTION DEPARTMENT

DIRECTOR OF PHOTOGRAPHY
In charge of lighting the film

SOUND RECORDIST
Captures clean dialogue and ambient sound

PRODUCTION DESIGNER
Controls the overall look of the movie

SUPERVISOR
Looks after stunts and practical effects

EDITOR
Makes sense of everything the director has shot

CAMERA OPERATOR
Often done by the DOP

BOOM OPERATOR
Keeps the mic close but out of shot

ART DIRECTOR
Realizes the production designer's vision

ASSISTANT

SOUND EDITOR
Oversees ADR, foley, and audio effects

FOCUS PULLER

PROPS   **MAKEUP**   **WARDROBE**   **SCENIC**

MUSIC SUPERVISOR
In charge of recording the film's score

PAINTER

CLAPPER LOADER
Also keeps a shot list

GRAPHIC DESIGNER
Oversees titling and publicity material

CARPENTER

KEY GRIP
Head of grip dept.

GAFFER
Head electrician

GRIP(S)
Light/camera riggers

DRIVER

BEST BOY

DRIVER

Who's who
Decide where your special interest and skills lie. Jobs are very specific, and don't overlap. Most divisions take on trainees, though not all the trainee roles are shown here.

On location
Collaborative skills are as important as technical skills when you are working as part of a small crew on a low-budget film.

Lo-no budget crew

In the low-no budget world, jobs overlap. Filmmakers working with an extremely limited budget are multi-skilled, and are good at working as part of a team. It goes without saying that shoots like this are intense and passionate affairs. Make sure you can work in these circumstances with your crew. Ideally your crew would include someone in charge of the camera and someone in charge of sound. Then there is you (the director). If you have the luxury of another person, then have a producer—someone who makes sure everything arrives at the right place at the right time.

Before you start shooting, it's a good idea to have someone in charge of the set or location (production designer/art director). The person taking this role can double as touch-up artist and makeup during the actual shoot. Of course, you could design, shoot, and record sound on your own. It's fun, but hard work.

At the lo-no budget end of moviemaking, on the whole, the fewer people you have working for you, the better it is. This is primarily an economic consideration because even if you aren't paying them, you have to at least feed them and cover their travel expenses.

If you can convince friends to help out willingly, without so much as a sandwich in return, that is another matter—and if they volunteer to work under those terms, better still. Of course, you don't want to surround yourself with deadwood either. When shooting guerrilla-style, you will need a small, tight-knit, multitasking crew that can work fast, anticipate situations, and solve problems.

As the size of the budget increases, so does the crew—and vice versa. You only have to watch the credits on a feature film to see the huge number of assistants, and assistants to the assistants, and so on ad infinitum. On small films it is best to get people to do a variety of tasks—it is good experience for them, and it makes for a tighter, more manageable team. Too much specialization results in an incredible amount of standing around on film sets, and if people are not busy, they will want to eat—or talk. The busier everyone is, the more

they will enjoy themselves and the greater their sense of achievement.

Start with friends

When you pick your crew, start with friends, or friends of friends. Acquaintance helps break the ice, and it has the added advantage of recommendation, although that isn't always a guarantee of ability. An alternative is to join a local theater group, which will give you access to all sorts of resources and skills that can easily be translated to movies. Only get people to do the jobs you can't actually do yourself, physically or technically. This is your show, so try to do as much as possible; but once you do take someone on, let her get on with the job—provided she's not messing up. The important things to get across are first, that you are in charge, and second, that you appreciate the help. Praise and thanks go a long way when there's no money.

Inspiration, Ideas, & Writing

The quickest way into the movie industry is to write a good script. All movies start with a screenplay. A film or new director will be discovered only if the script is outstanding.

We are going to look at ways in which bold, fresh, and original ideas can be generated—ideas that no one has thought of yet, but that the film business is looking for. With the right idea (one that you are really excited about) you need to learn how to write it for the camera.

Finally, remember the little secret of movies: You don't get paid for writing a screenplay, you only get paid for selling it. Let's develop a realistic plan for writing and selling your script.

How do you come up with ideas?

An idea is the seed from which a screenplay grows. There are many ways to produce ideas for a movie. The goal is to come up with an idea that you like and can work with in order to maintain your enthusiasm about the project.

Influences and emulation

Have you ever seen a movie and right afterward thought "I'd like to make a movie like that"? George Lucas' first *Star Wars* movie influenced quite a few directors, from Kevin Smith to low-budget director Scooter McCrae. While these directors never made a *Star Wars*, they were successful in making their own unique brand of movies. Seeing *Star Wars* at a young age kickstarted their desire to make a movie and similarly to affect viewers. In fact, Kevin Smith spoofed *Star Wars* in both *Jay and Silent Bob Strike Back* and *Zack & Miri*. And while Lucas' film was a huge influence, Scooter McCrae veered off in a completely different direction with horror movies *Shatter Dead* and *Sixteen Tongues*.

Books

Have you ever read a book that you thought would make a great movie? The idea is already there, so it's a matter of adapting the prose to a screenplay. *The Talented Mr. Ripley* by Patricia Highsmith was made into a movie twice, first as *Purple Noon*

and then as the 1998 movie starring Matt Damon. *The Body Snatchers* by Jack Finney was made into a movie four times. There are also numerous movies based on characters from books that are now in the public domain, such as *Dracula*, *Frankenstein*, and *Sherlock Holmes*. In 2008 there were three different movie adaptations of Jules Verne's *Journey to the Center of the Earth*.

Real life

Have you, or anyone you know, ever had an interesting experience that you thought would make the basis for a great movie, or read about a situation in the newspaper that would lend itself to film? If it's interesting and you think it can be a basis for a movie, write it down. Examples of movies based on real life range from the Charlize Theron movie *Monster* to the Stephen King adaptation *Stand By Me*.

Once you come up with the idea that you like, it's time to expand upon it and determine if it's a "high concept" or "low-concept" movie.

High concept vs. low concept

"High concept" movies can be described in one sentence and usually have simple characters and predictable situations. They have broad themes that have universal appeal, such as *Star Wars*. They are easier to pitch. These types of movies usually have star names attached, such as Bruce Willis for the *Die Hard* movies. The aim of a "high concept" idea is to be popular. Movies like *King Kong* and *The Babysitter* are high concept. The movie can be summed up in five words, such as with Eric Red's *The Hitcher*, "Never pick up a stranger," and the concept can also

Monster movie
Monster, which won Charlize Theron an Oscar, is one of the "based on real life" genre. There are all sorts of legal implications in making a bio-pic; however, newspaper stories can be a great source of inspiration, and reality can often be stranger than fiction.

be in the title, such as *I Married a Monster From Outer Space* or the Jim Carrey vehicle *Yes Man*. You immediately know what the movie is about. "High concept" ideas are easier to sell.

"Low concept" movies cannot be summed up so easily and are more complex and demand more thought and work from the audience. These movies can be anything from a mystery to a character study. If you are looking for a movie with a "plot," then it is probably "low concept." Examples of this are *The Prestige* and any M. Night Shyamalan movie. It's best to remember that "high" and "low" concept doesn't refer to the quality of the idea or the movie; it's simply a way of succinctly describing the idea.

What is a screenplay?

A screenplay is the "blueprint" or "instruction manual" of the movie. It is the detailed content of a film numbered into scenes or sequences which contains descriptions of what will happen, technical directions for the camera or editing, and all the dialogue that the actors will say.

Sum it up!

Can you come up with three ideas for a movie that you can sum up in a few words? For example:

★ *Camelot 3000*
King Arthur in outer space.

★ *Dahmer's Daughter*
A woman is the unlikely offspring of a serial killer.

★ *Runaway With Elvis*
Teen goes on a road trip with a burned-out Elvis Presley.

Writing summaries

Watch three films you think are high concept. See if you can write a one-line summary of each. For example:

★ *My Super Ex-Girlfriend*
A man breaks up with the secret identity of a super-heroine.

★ *Pearl Harbor*
Soldiers deal with the Japanese attack on Pearl Harbor.

MUST-SEE MOVIES

★ *SPEED* (1994)
Key Players: Director Jan de Bont; writer Graham Yost
A bus is set to explode if its speed drops below 50 mph (80 kph). Classic example of a high-concept film.

★ *GHOST WORLD* (2001)
Key Players: Director Terry Zwigoff; writer Daniel Clowes
The plot of this film is based on an underground graphic novel.

Identifying movies

See if you can identify the movie from this one-line summary? For example:

1. *"Jaws in space"*
2. "Romeo and Juliet on junk"
3. *"Giant ape kidnaps beautiful blonde"*
4. *"High Noon in space"*
5. *"Immobile protagonist witnesses murder from his window"*

ANSWERS: **1.** *Alien.* **2.** *Panic In Needle Park.* **3.** *King Kong.* **4.** *Outland.* **5.** *Rear Window.*

Masters of the nail-biter
Alfred Hitchcock, like Stephen King, could take a simple idea and turn it into a nail-biting thriller. In the case of *Rear Window*, a man confined to a room is looking out of his window with binoculars. The film's concept was recently reimagined and updated as *Disturbia*, starring Shia LaBeouf.

What is story structure?

Structure is the term that film industry people use to describe the way a story unfolds. The most common structure is a three-act story.

A three-act screenplay has a beginning, a middle, and an end. On the facing page is a paradigm invented by the highly respected script doctor and theorist Syd Field. However, a three-act story structure has several flaws:

■ It is based on theater, where the curtain actually falls. Of course, this doesn't happen in cinema.
■ It allows for just three major plot points. Most successful movies have up to 15 plot points (see below).

■ It is very rigid, and doesn't allow for more complex story forms.

Even so, a three-act story structure is a good place to start. But learn to move on from there as soon as you can. If you are an intuitive storyteller, the way you tell your story will create its own structure.

Star Wars: plot points

Syd Field's three-act paradigm can be broken down into further plot points as shown here using *Star Wars* as an example. George Lucas' screenplay was inspired by the mythical story structure as described by Joseph Campbell, which lays out specific plot points within the three-act structure. A single page of film script equals approximately one minute of film time.

PP = plot point

PLOT POINT 1
Page 1: time, place, setting
Set in the future on a starship, we see two robots, C3PO and R2D2, in the middle of battle mayhem. The war is between the Empire, a tyrannical government set on oppression, and the Rebellion, adversaries of the Empire who want peace restored to the galaxy.

PLOT POINT 3
Page 10: the plan
After being rescued by Luke Skywalker, the two robots convey their mission to the lonely farm boy.

PLOT POINT 5
Page 45: second reversal
Luke finds a hermit in the desert. Obi-Wan Kenobi used to be a Jedi, a legendary warrior of the old Republic. Obi-Wan tells Luke that he trained his father in the way of the Jedi, and that Darth Vader, the evil warrior of the Empire, killed Luke's father. Luke is given his father's lightsaber, the weapon of the Jedi.

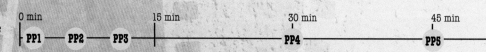

0 min   ⊢ **PP1** — **PP2** — **PP3** ⊣   15 min   30 min   **PP4**   45 min   **PP5**

PLOT POINT 2
Page 3: theme
In order to escape the laser gun shootouts aboard the ship, the two robots stow away. A lady in a white gown gives R2D2 an encoded message and a mission to deliver it to a certain Obi-Wan Kenobi. C3PO insists that "We'll be smashed to pieces!" which is what the film is really about. They launch from the starship on an escape pod and land on the neighboring planet of Tatooine.

PLOT POINT 4
Page 30: first reversal
The orphan Luke announces that he wants a life full of adventure; that he wants to leave the farm and help the robots in their quest. His request is denied by his uncle, who sees too much of Luke's father in him. Luke gets into his Landspeeder and rides away.

PLOT POINT 6
Page 60: point of no return
Luke returns home to the farm to find his aunt and uncle burned alive. Luke can no longer go back to his life as it was on Page 10. Luke is catapulted into a mission to help Obi-Wan in his quest to save the princess, the woman in white who gave R2D2 the message at the beginning.

How Syd Field's Paradigm works

The opening act introduces us to the characters and setting of the film, with a major plot event about 20 minutes into the film. The setup is needed to capture the viewer's attention. The second act is where most of the action (confrontation) takes place, building to a climax just before the final act, which is the resolution of the story, often the familiar Hollywood happy ending. A strong ending is needed as this is the last thing your audience will see and remember most.

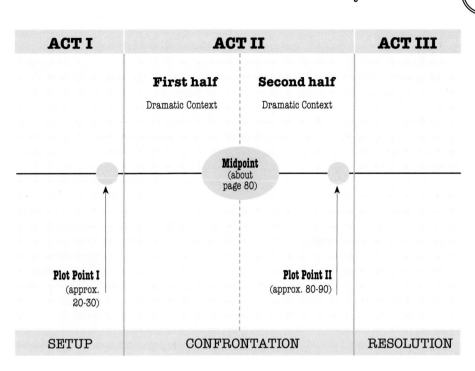

PLOT POINT 7
Page 75: the big gloom
Luke and Obi-Wan find Han Solo, a mischievous and hardened pilot, and his hairy friend Chewbacca, who agree to fly them off Tatooine. They are forced to land in the Death Star, the Empire's ultimate weapon, powerful enough to destroy an entire planet.

After rescuing Princess Leia, Luke, Han, Chewy, and Leia fall into a trash compactor pit, which grows smaller every second. With the walls closing in on them, they fear they will not be able to escape and continue their mission to get Leia back to the Rebel Alliance base, where she is one of the leaders. R2D2 finds the programming for the trash compactor and stops the device just before our heroes are squished to death.

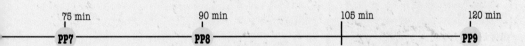

PLOT POINT 8
Page 90: the final battle
When Luke is recruited among a group of pilots in an attempt to destroy the Death Star, he makes the decision to become an active player in the Rebel Alliance. Han takes the money promised to him, and leaves dishonorably. As the pilots take flight and storm the trenches of the Death Star, Luke is the last hope for the mission, as all others have failed. Han Solo returns to the scene to fight off the enemy so Luke can carry out his mission. He fires two shots and hits his target.

PLOT POINT 9
Page 120: resolution
Luke Skywalker, Han Solo, Chewbacca, R2D2, and C3PO are rewarded with medals for their efforts in the Rebel cause. Leia leads the ceremony, and the movie ends in celebration.

Analyze the action

Watch two of your favorite films with a stopwatch. Every time something happens, write it down, along with a reference to the time. One page of screenplay, properly typed and formatted, roughly equals a minute of screen time. See if you can identify the key scenes. Analyze the action points and look for any patterns or similarities. Here are two examples to get you started.

A still from *Knocked Up*, starring Seth Rogen and Katherine Heigl.

Knocked Up (2007)

16 minutes: The two main characters meet at a bar, get drunk, and have unprotected sex.

22 minutes: They both realize that being together is a mistake.

32 minutes: She tells him that she's pregnant with his child.

62 minutes: He proposes, but she says she has to think about it.

82 minutes: They break up and stop seeing each other.

110 minutes: They get back together when she gives birth.

The Evil Dead (1981)

3 minutes: On their way to a secluded cabin, friends almost become involved in a deadly car wreck.

15 minutes: They find a trapdoor in the cabin that leads down to ancient artifacts.

26 minutes: One of the women is attacked in the woods by a demon.

33 minutes: The friends try to escape, but they are trapped because the bridge is destroyed.

36 minutes: The woman who was attacked is possessed and tries to kill the others. They lock her in the basement.

45 minutes: Another woman gets possessed and is killed by the men.

51 minutes: The last woman is possessed by a demon.

60 minutes: One of the two men dies and the surviving guy has to try to destroy the last demon.

78 minutes: Final confrontation between the last survivor and the demon.

Sketch out a structure

Come up with an idea for a structure based on one of these ideas:

- **Days of the week:** On Monday this happens, on Tuesday this, etc.

- **Common experience:** In the first part of the story, everyone is waking up, while in the last part of the story everyone is having dinner or going to bed.

- **The year:** A story that spans a year, or a story that repeats at the same time each year—now, one year later, or 10 years later, and so on…

- **The seasons:** Shakespeare often used the four seasons as a structural device. Combine them with symbolism, i.e., summer—growth, winter—death. Try mixing these up for a different effect.

- **Nature:** The concentric rings spreading from a pebble dropped in a pond, or the branching of a tree limb can provide inspiration for your story structure.

Build a framework

Write a sentence to describe the action in each of the 6 to 9 key scenes of your film. For example, if you have chosen the "days of the week" structure (see project 5), start with (1) Monday morning and work through the week, as below. Focus on the characters and what they want.

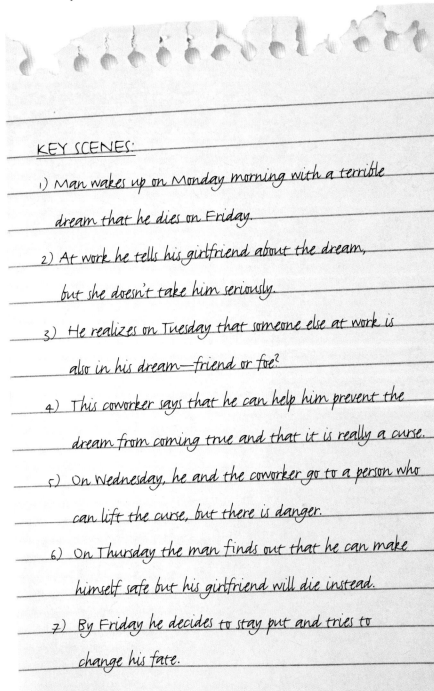

KEY SCENES:

1) Man wakes up on Monday morning with a terrible dream that he dies on Friday.

2) At work he tells his girlfriend about the dream, but she doesn't take him seriously.

3) He realizes on Tuesday that someone else at work is also in his dream—friend or foe?

4) This coworker says that he can help him prevent the dream from coming true and that it is really a curse.

5) On Wednesday, he and the coworker go to a person who can lift the curse, but there is danger.

6) On Thursday the man finds out that he can make himself safe but his girlfriend will die instead.

7) By Friday he decides to stay put and tries to change his fate.

MUST-SEE MOVIES

★ *THE CRYING GAME* (1992)
Key player: Director: Neil Jordan; screenplay Neil Jordan
Radical depiction of the unseen laws of desire. You won't see it coming.

★ *RUSHMORE* (1998)
Key Players: Director Wes Anderson; writer Wes Anderson and Owen Wilson
The film follows Max Fisher over the course of one year in high school.

Involving chance

Director Christopher Nolan claims that when he and his brother, Jonathan, wrote *Memento*, they sketched out the key scenes on the back of a deck of playing cards and then threw them down the stairs, creating the unusual structure of the movie. Why don't you do the same and see what happens? For example, using the key scenes you drafted in the previous project, reorder them, as in the example shown on this page.

At work the man tells his girlfriend about the dream, but she doesn't take him seriously.

He realizes that someone else at work is also in his dream—friend or foe?

The man finds out that he can make himself safe but his girlfriend will die instead.

Man wakes up on Monday morning with a terrible dream that he dies on Friday.

He decides to stay put and tries to change his fate.

A coworker says that he can help prevent the dream from coming true and that it is really a curse.

He and the coworker go to a person who can lift the curse, but there is danger.

Creating memorable characters

Here are some of the formulas, tools, and techniques that professional screenwriters employ to develop and create characters—characters that stick with you long after the movie is over.

Think of the last time you went to a movie you really loved. When you woke up the next morning, was it the first thing you thought of? And what did you remember most? The plot points—or the people you met on the screen? If you've seen a great movie in the theater and then watched it again three months or more later on DVD, did you say to yourself, "I remember that Jim Carrey character, but I don't remember that scene?" People watch movies to meet interesting and compelling characters.

Create the cast for your movie

Eventually, you will be holding an audition for your movie, but first you have to decide the roles each character will play so that you get the right kind of actors to come to your audition. Most commercially successful movies have three or four main characters. There may be lots of other characters, but you should always start with the main characters. The projects on these two pages will help you.

PROJECT 8

Four-point opposition

Start by developing the characters to suit the four main roles. Successful stories often have three or four main characters in conflict. Create conflict by making sure each character is as different as possible from the others. Contrasts like this create stress and tension whenever they are together. And good storytelling is the result. One traditional, high-concept example of this can be seen within the *Spider-Man* franchise: The hero is Peter Parker; the opponent, Norman Osbourne. These two work in opposition to one another with Parker (as Spider-Man) repeatedly foiling Osbourne's schemes.

Hero or protagonist

The person we root for, in this case, Peter Parker, through whose eyes we see the story. He is the person we feel sad for if he doesn't get what he wants.

Ally opponent

At the start of the movie, this character is an ally of the Hero, but then switches allegiance. Have you ever had a best friend who stabbed you in the back? In Parker's life it is Harry Osbourne who plays this role.

Opponent ally

At the start of the movie, this character is strongly aligned to the Opponent, but then decides to switch his friendship to the Hero; like Flash Thompson in the film

Internal struggles
Spider-Man was the teenage everyman with whom the audience could identify. The movie brought to life the internal conflicts between the geeky Peter Parker alongside the responsibilities of his heroic alter ego.

Opponent or antagonist

Not necessarily the bad guy (that's too clichéd), but the person who most stands in the way of what the Hero wants. A classic example is Norman Osbourne, Parker's nemesis.

Getting to know you

PROJECT 9

Use an index card like this to get to know your main characters. The object is to get to know each of the main characters as well as you know your best friend. Start by writing the role of each character at the top of a separate card.

GENDER: Female
ROLE: Ally Opponent
AGE: Sue is 30 years old.
SCHOOL: She has a Master's in Fine Art.
HOBBIES: Fishing
FIRST LOVE: While she has had many boyfriends, she has never been in love.
JOB\JOB ASPIRATION: Secretary at a public relations company
PARENTS: Parents died in a boating accident.
PARENTS' OCCUPATIONS: Ghosts
BEST FRIEND: Her best friend is her cat.
FAVORITE MUSIC: Nirvana
DISLIKES: Country music and men with beards

GENDER: Male
ROLE: Hero
AGE: Kev is 20-something.
SCHOOL: He flunked out because he was too busy chasing girls.
HOBBIES: Football, football, and football.
FIRST LOVE: Despite his bragging, never had a girlfriend.
JOB/JOB ASPIRATION: Doorman for building.
PARENTS: Kev's parents are still together.
PARENTS' OCCUPATIONS: Father an electrician; Mother is a healthcare professional
BEST FRIEND: Bruce hates sport, and is a computer geek.
FAVORITE MUSIC: Folk music
DISLIKES: Loud music and girls who wear too much mascara

Testing, testing

PROJECT 10

Think back to the last movie you saw and each of the characters in it. Choose one. Would you like to spend two hours in a dark, empty room with him or her? If yes, why? If not, why not?

Flesh out your characters

PROJECT 11

Think back to your relationships with your friends and family. Choose someone you know and ask yourself these questions:

- What are his strong points?
- What do you find irritating about him?
- What is the thing that gets him out of bed in the morning?
- What is his big dream?
- If you wanted to hurt him, what would you do?

Now ask these questions of each of your main characters. Write down the answers. Some examples are given below.

JOE:
1. If he says he will do something, he will.
2. He asks too many questions.
3. He loves his job; he doesn't want to be late.
4. His dream is to move to Florida.
5. To hurt his feelings, you would tell him he isn't very smart.

DEBBIE:
1. She is tough.
2. She doesn't eat the crusts on pizzas.
3. She is eternally optimistic.
4. She wants to own her own antique business.
5. To hurt her feelings, ask her if she's gained weight.

AL:
1. He is a good driver.
2. He talks aloud and swears at other drivers.
3. He needs to get to work to make money.
4. His big dream is to own a boat.
5. To hurt his feelings, tell him that he's lazy.

JOSEPHINE:
1. She is a good listener.
2. She's too intrusive.
3. She is a light sleeper, so getting up in the morning isn't a problem.
4. Her big dream is to get married.
5. To hurt her feelings, tell her that she'll never find her "soul mate."

Develop your characters

You have created your main characters. Now you have to develop them, and make them compelling to the viewer. There are a number of professional storytelling tools and techniques that you can use to achieve this.

See also:
Creating memorable characters, page 20

The "plan"

Your main character should want something specific that is tracked over the course of the story—let's call it the "plan." Choosing the right plan is probably the single most important step in creating a great character.

Here's a character plan that's too vague to work: "I want to move out of the city." Why? There has to be a compelling reason that motivates and drives the character's actions. Maybe this is better: "I have to leave the city by noon tomorrow or… [create a dire consequence if your hero fails to achieve his goal]." The strength of this plan is that there is a precise moment when the audience can see whether the main character achieves his or her goal.

Introduce character flaws

Give your hero two problems to solve at the same time. The outer problem (which is what the audience sees) is the specific goal that your hero wants to achieve over the course of the story. The inner problem is an emotional issue with which the hero wrestles. In real life, we all suffer character flaws, whether these be a psychological weakness, such as tardiness, procrastination, insecurity, or lack of confidence, or a moral weakness, such as lying, stealing, cheating, or jealousy. Make your characters human by making them flawed.

Stereotypes

We all tend to pigeonhole people into boxes. Stereotypical characters, as such, are probably the worst type of character to put into a movie. But if you use your audience's preconceptions of a stereotype as a shorthand tool to introduce the character, you can then twist the audience's perception of the character.

Traits

Successful screenwriters use a tool called magnification to make their characters pop off the screen. They take stereotypical characters, and then add traits that break the mold. For example, a bald, short, fat banker, wearing a three-piece suit, who loves acid jazz, or a dirty, addicted, homeless person who is depressed and a loser but has a working knowledge of medieval history.

The role of the opponent

The opponent is the least understood character in storytelling. Often thought of as the "bad guy," in fact opponent characters are not bad at all. They have their own dreams, strengths, and weaknesses. In a truly great story, the hero is opposed by an opponent who is stronger, braver, smarter, or more cunning than the main character. Only then is the outcome uncertain.

Identify the stereotype

List 10 characters by occupation whom you might like to see in a movie—builder, teacher, and so on. Then list the stereotypical traits for each character. There are three main types of traits.

1. **Physical traits**
   (e.g., tall, weak, deformed, blonde)

2. **Sociological trait**
   (e.g., housed, homeless, employed, jobless)

3. **Psychological traits**
   (e.g., paranoid, arrogant, honest)

Banker:
Bald, short, dressed in a three-piece pinstripe suit, vindictive

Homeless person:
Dirty, addicted, loner, depressed

Rich girl:
Curvy, heiress, pathological liar

Adding unusual traits

Go back to your list of 10 characters from project 12 and give each of them an unusual trait.

CHARACTER	STEREOTYPICAL TRAIT	UNUSUAL TRAIT
1) Engineer	anal, neat freak, country music fan	has Tourette's syndrome
2) Yoga instructor	blonde, flaky	avid hunter
3) Construction worker	strong, simple	cooks
4) Doctor	intelligent, older	gambler
5) Dentist	nerdy, depressed, short	collector
6) Cashier	high school dropout, young	nudist
7) Garbage collector	uneducated, strong	writer
8) Teacher	wears glasses, spinster, strict	alcoholic
9) FBI agent	handsome, wears a dark suit, tall	stutterer
10) Baker	overweight, missing two fingers	rocker

Magnification

Hollywood loves to take an unusual trait and magnify it to the breaking point. Go back to your list of 10 characters and magnify at least one trait per character.

CHARACTER	TRAIT MAGNIFIED
1) Engineer	He is stalking a certain country singer.
2) Yoga instructor	Decides to go on a bear hunt in Alaska.
3) Construction worker	Wants to open a restaurant.
4) Doctor	Is deep in debt to some unsavory characters.
5) Dentist	Discovers that one of his comics is worth millions.
6) Cashier	Gets in trouble at a nudist colony.
7) Garbage collector	Sells book and becomes best-selling novelist.
8) Teacher	Starts having blackouts in class.
9) FBI agent	Starts to stutter when he's in grave danger.
10) Baker	His garage rock band becomes famous.

HEROINE:	OPPONENT:
quiet	obnoxious
plain	beautiful
plump	tall and slim
aloof	popular
intelligent	genius
blonde	brunette
working-class	wealthy
nervous	confident

Clash of characters

List the main character traits of your protagonist and then make sure that your opponent character contradicts or is superior in every single one (see the example at left).

MUST-SEE MOVIES

★ *THE SHAWSHANK REDEMPTION* (1994)
Key Player: Director: Frank Darabont
Every one of the characters in this film, from Andy Dufresne to the young convict Tommy, is beautifully drawn.

★ *CROUCHING TIGER, HIDDEN DRAGON* (2000)
Key Players: Director: Ang Lee;
Screenplay: Huis Lang Wang
Yu Shu-lien is a warrior, a magnificent swordswoman and a wonderfully strong character, equal to the male lead.

How to write for the camera

A picture is worth a thousand words, and so writing for movies means being able to create movie pictures with your words. Here are some basic rules.

You can only include what you physically see on the screen. There is no point writing "Frank feels down." How would you show that visually? It's impossible. So think about how you can show that Frank is depressed. For instance, "Frank wipes a tear from his face."

If your screenplay has too many interior thoughts, perhaps the story is better suited to a novel or a poem.

A writer's job is to describe all the action seen on the screen. And that means everything that you hear and see on the screen. If you just write "car chase," it's a cop out.

A page of screenplay is a minute of screen time. You may be visualizing a car chase that will last for a minute, but your description is indicating that it will be over in a few seconds. Ask yourself: How long is the scene? Is it day or night? Where do you see the chase? How fast is it going? Which characters are in the scene? What are the near misses? When does the car go around the corner on two wheels? Everything you picture in your mind must be written down.

When you start writing a new scene, sit back and try to imagine yourself sitting in a theater in front of a blank screen. What do you see?

Screenplays must be submitted in the correct format, or the industry personnel you are pursuing will ignore your submission.

Screenplay rules

■ Length
Each script page is generally considered to be a minute of screen time.

■ Dialogue
Unlike in plays and novels, dialogue in a script is as short and economical as possible. Many writers see dialogue as another form of action, putting characters at odds, driving the plotline.

■ Don't use camera directions
This strategy helps to make the script more readable, as camera descriptions are often clumsy and break up the flow.

■ And also...
Don't number your scenes. Scripts are given scene numbers only when they are budgeted and scheduled to be shot. Spell out two-digit numbers, personal titles, and indications of time. Do not hyphenate long words from one line to the next or break a sentence from one page to the next. When a long passage of dialogue needs to be continued onto another page, type (MORE) at the character cue tab and then (CONTINUED) after the character cue on the following page.

PROJECT 16

See how the experts write action

List your three favorite action sequences and watch them. Now get the screenplay from *www.imsdb.com*. Read the passages and study how these professional writers have written the scene. Below is a still and fragment from the script from *Saving Private Ryan*.

```
FADE IN:

EXT. OMAHA BEACH—NORMANDY—DAWN

The ROAR OF NAVAL GUNS continues but now WE SEE THEM FIRING.
Huge fifteen inch guns.

SWARM OF LANDING CRAFT

Heads directly into a nightmare.  MASSIVE EXPLOSIONS from
German artillery shells and mined obstacles tear apart the
beach. Hundreds of German machine guns, loaded with tracers,
pour out a red snowstorm of bullets.

OFFSHORE SUPERIMPOSITION:

        OMAHA BEACH,
  NORMANDY June 6, 1940

        0600 HOURS.

HUNDREDS OF LANDING
CRAFT.

Each holding thirty men,
near the beaches.

THE CLIFFS.

At the far end of
the beach, a ninety-
foot cliff.  Topped
by bunkers. Ringed by
fortified machine gun
nests. A clear line-
of-fire down the entire
beach.

TEN LANDING CRAFT.

Make their way toward
the base of the
```

Still from the opening scene of "Saving Private Ryan."

How to format a screenplay

If you don't follow the simple formatting rules, you will make a script look amateurish. Practice laying out a sample script page.

Capitalization
When characters are first introduced their names should be capitalized. Thereafter, in descriptive passages, the names appear in upper and lower case.

Scene description
Always double-spaced down from the scene heading, the scene description indicates in the most economical terms what the setting is, who the characters are, and what action is taking place.

Indents
Different depth indents allow the action, speech, and characters' names to be distinguished easily from each other.

3" indent

> COREY (cont'd)
> one suitcase. That leaves you out of it. I'm going to shoot Blazer's mouth shut.

She fondles an ashtray

EXT. JERSEY STREET—DAWN

But BLAZER isn't available right now, because he's rollerblading toward the flapping door of a circus tent.

CUT TO:

Cut to
Some writers never use "cut to," arguing that transition is implied by moving from one scene to another.

Scene headings
Scene headings indicate whether the location is an interior (INT.) or exterior (EXT.), the location, and whether it is day or night.

INT.   TENT—DAY

1½" indent

> Blazer glides into the tent and comes to a perfect stop right under the nose of PHIL, the Balloon King. It's taken the FAT LADY about two seconds to realize where she's seen his face before.

4" indent

> PHIL
> What do you want?

His voice breaks out in an audible sweat.

> BLAZER
> I'm looking for a couple of hire-wire boys—Frank Hillski and Paul Bertoli.

"Character cue"
This is the name given to the character who speaks the line of dialogue that follows.

The swinging overhead light shatters into a million pieces.

3½" indent

> BLAZER
> (continuing)
> I want to show them new ways to fly.

12-pt Courier typeface
Screenplays and teleplays are written in 12-point Courier, which has evolved from the old manual typewriter's typeface.

Set the scene

PROJECT 18

Look around the room you are in right now. Describe the scene in screenplay format. Pretend that you are the actor in the scene. See if you can find the action, the movement, and the emotion of the scene (see the example, right).

INT. LIVING ROOM—NIGHT

A blizzard can be seen through the large glass window. A man stands stock still in the center of the room as if waiting for something. The overhead light flickers, and we can hear the sound of the wind outside. He starts when his large dog jumps on him and begins barking.

Break down the action

PROJECT 19

Think about a time when you traveled to a new city and had to find an address. Describe the journey from the station or airport. Describe step-by-step how you found the address. Show us when you stopped to look at a map or studied a street sign until you found the right door (see the example, right).

INT. AIRPORT—DAY

A man hurries down the crowded stairway of the airport lobby, down to luggage. There is a wide variety of people, and he's almost lost in the bustle.

EXT. AIRPORT—DAY

He gets in the unbelievably long line to wait for a taxi. There are signs along the way that say, "if someone offers to give you a ride they are not an authorized taxi." The woman in front of him, who is on her cell phone, keeps banging into his knees with her wheeled suitcase. He tries to back up, but there are people behind him.

INT. CAB—DAY

He gets into the cab, a newer model that looks like a minivan, and shows the written address to the cab driver, who shakes his head.

EXT. CAB—DAY

The cab peels away from the curb and into city traffic.

EXT. VARIOUS MOVING SHOTS OF NEW YORK CITY—DAY

This is a montage sequence of various shots, from the point of view of the side window, of driving down the highway toward the city, crossing the Queensboro Bridge, seeing pedestrians and other cars go by.

EXT. BUILDING—DAY

The cab nearly drives past an old brownstone apartment building, slams on its brakes, and backs up a dozen feet, almost running into a car coming down the one-way street. The car honks as the passenger pays the cabbie and gets out. The cab driver almost pulls away before the passenger shuts the door.

MUST-SEE MOVIES

★ *ALIENS* (1986)
Key Players: Director: James Cameron;
Writers: Dan O'Bannon and Ronald Shusett
Massacre in space; a superbly written yarn.

★ *KILL BILL: VOLUME 1* (2003)
Key Players: Director and Writer: Quentin Tarantino
Blends genres and action styles in telling the story of a woman spurned.

Action, not description

Scenes start with a line, denoting inside or outside, day or night. The trick is not to bore the reader by completely describing the setting. This could lead to an overwritten scene, which is one of the fatal flaws of scene writing. Instead, describe the one or two details that give us a clue, and let the reader's imagination fill in the rest.

Describing the scene

```
INT. OFFICE—DAY
```

Sometimes this is enough information for the production designer to decide what furniture and what artwork should be used. Other times, you need to write some additional information:

```
INT. OFFICE—DAY
Water leaks from
the radiator.
```

Now the designer has some more information that might spark an idea of what the set is to look like. You do not describe things; you describe things happening.

Attention to details

The details you include will greatly impact how the production team recreates your set.

```
INT. OFFICE—DAY
Paper cups and
empty pizza
boxes litter
the desk.
```

```
INT. OFFICE—DAY
A vase of lilies
sits next to the
telephone.
```

Two offices are described above. These are two very different rooms. Which one do you want in your movie? It's up to you, the writer. Carefully select details that imply other details.

Write movement

If you want to describe an actor's movements, you can bury the description so it isn't so obvious:

```
INT. OFFICE—DAY
Frank swipes the
coffee cups and
pizza boxes off his
desk.
```

Write the emotion of the scene

Don't describe how something looks. That is the job of the production designer. The casting director will decide how the actors look. Your job as a writer is to describe the attitude and the feeling of the scene:

```
INT. OFFICE—DAY
Sparks leap from the
socket. A ceiling fan
whirls. Moths bang
against the windowpane.
This place looks like it
hasn't seen an ounce of
decency for years.
```

Keep it brief

Don't overwrite. If you are describing a house as: "a Colonial house built in the late 1780s with six windows, a brick chimney, and paint peeling off the clapboards" it is too much detail. Instead, write: "Rundown mansion."

Developing a strong personal style

Your goal as a writer is to develop a strong and distinctive style. Familiarize yourself with the work of professional writers by reading and rereading their scripts. Your job is to write word pictures that will inspire everyone on the set, from the lowliest walk-on extra to the props buyer, the director, and the actors.

Make a storyboard

Materials
When choosing drawing materials, consider speed and reproducibility.

Once you have written a concept or script for a film, the next step is to make a storyboard. A storyboard visually tells the story, panel by panel. Professional storyboard artists or production illustrators, like Tim Burgard, will develop their own unique style.

Key storyboard elements

1. What characters are in the frame, and how are they moving?
2. What the characters are saying to each other.
3. Timeline: lets us know how much time has passed since the last frame.
4. The passage of time between the last frame of the storyboard and the current one.
5. Where's the camera? Close or far away? Is it moving?

Why make a storyboard?

Creating a storyboard will help you plan your film out shot by shot and will allow you easily to make changes to your story before you start filming. You will also be able to talk about your film and show your storyboard to other people to get valuable feedback and advice.

How do I make a storyboard?

The simplest storyboards are drawn in pen or pencil. You can also take photos, cut out pictures from magazines, or use a computer to make a storyboard. Drawings don't have to be fancy—the best results are when you spend just a few minutes drawing each frame. Use basic shapes, stick figures, and simple backgrounds. If you draw your storyboard frames on index cards, you can rearrange them to move parts of the story around.

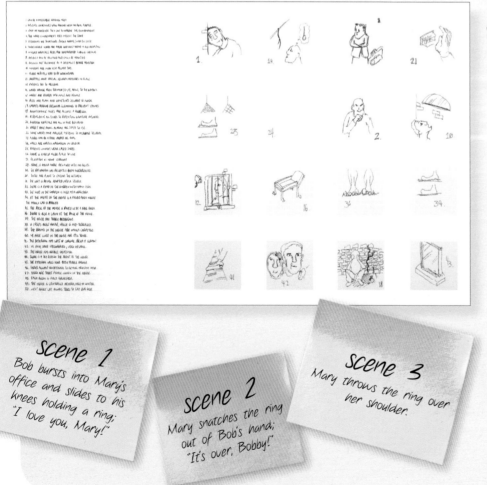

PROJECT **20**

Sticky-note storyboards

■ Get a piece of white poster board, at least 20 x 30 in. (40 x 60 cm) and a packet of sticky notes. Label each sticky note with the scene number and a brief sketch describing the scene.

■ Plan for four or five rows of sticky notes horizontally across the board, leaving room for writing text below each one. Write the text of your script in pencil, placing your sticky-note images above the appropriate words. You can move notes or take them out altogether, and you can easily erase the text as well.

scene 1
Bob bursts into Mary's office and slides to his knees holding a ring; "I love you, Mary!"

scene 2
Mary snatches the ring out of Bob's hand; "It's over, Bobby!"

scene 3
Mary throws the ring over her shoulder.

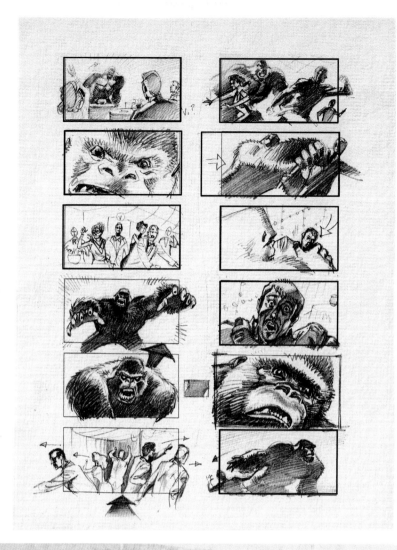

Professional storyboard from a film
Initial sketches for the movie *Mighty Joe Young* for Disney. Tim Burgard will go on to annotate the sketches with important information ready for filming, the next stage.

PROJECT 22

Use mini-models

Position toy characters in relation to each other and see if you can imagine the shot. Or use art school mannequins. Position the mannequins and take a digital photograph, import images into a computer, and size them before printing storyboard frames.

PROJECT 21

Simple storyboard

Your task is to make a basic storyboard using nothing more elaborate than stick figures. The challenge here is not to get bogged down trying to finesse your drawings.

PROJECT 23

Find free storyboard templates

There are various blank storyboard templates in different screen ratios that you can download from the Internet. Have a look for yourself. Print off dozens of templates because you'll need plenty. These sheets, once they are filled in, can be bound into a folder to avoid losing them.

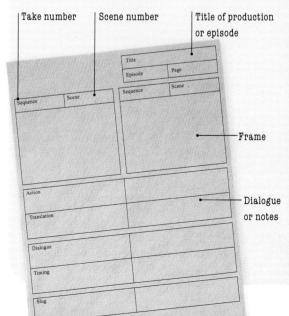

Take number   Scene number   Title of production or episode

Frame

Dialogue or notes

Selling your screenplay

You don't make money writing a screenplay—you only get paid when you sell it. You are always in the first draft of a screenplay until you sell it. Never send a script to someone unless they ask for it.

The golden rules of salesmanship

When you want to get what you want there are some simple tips that can help:

1 Never say a number.

Go into the negotiations with a realistic minimum budget, but never reveal it. Tell them what you want to do and let them figure out an amount based on their experience. It could be a lot more than you expect. If it doesn't match your minimum then walk away. If they want it, they will chase you.

2 Never go to money.

Going to their offices can be intimidating for you. Always meet in a neutral place of your choosing, where there will be fewer distractions, even if it means buying coffee or lunch.

3 If you don't ask, you don't get.

Show you have confidence in what you are selling by asking for a deal right away. Ask questions like, "I hear you are interested in my film" and "Are you still interested in thrillers, as I have one of those too?" If they say yes, then ask them to give you a check.

The query letter

A query letter should be as succinct as possible. The object is to get a meeting with someone interested in buying your screenplay.

First paragraph
Who you are. What your day job is, even if it is boring.

Synopsis
Your brief synopsis: in as few words as possible a summary of the storyline.

Find out the name of the Development Executive, and address him or her by name, using the full name. Don't try to be chummy.

Kitty Kirbsticks
33 Mean Street
Townsville, CA 22346

Tel: 555 333 333
Email: kitty@film.org

Xavier Butler
Development Executive
Film Production Company Inc.
Revolution Rd.
Anytown, PA 19100

December 16, 2009

Identify and name the genre

Dear Xavier Butler,

I am a recent film school graduate who is currently working as an intern for a film festival. I have written a feature-length romantic-comedy screenplay, which may be of interest to you.

It is the story of a small-town guy who promises to take his girlfriend to Europe, but he's broke. The twist is she is blind. With the help of his best friends, an Italian from the local pizzeria and the Greek guy next door, he decides to fake a trip to Europe without leaving town.

I would like to submit my script for your consideration.

I look forward to hearing from you in the near future.

Kitty Kirbsticks

Last 2 lines:
Explain what you are submitting

The pitch meeting

When you spark the interest of a producer or agent, he or she will want to meet you one-on-one at a "pitch meeting." At this meeting, you will be given the opportunity to impart your enthusiasm for the project to producers with money, or to talented directors, actors, and crew who want to make your film.

There are three parts to a pitch meeting: the beginning (the "schmooze"), the middle (the pitch), and the end.

During the schmooze, each party assesses the other and tries to decide whether they get along. It's a bit like when you meet up with friends and ask how their day was. But rather than discussing boring things like the weather, go prepared with background information on the person or the company, which you can find on that person's website or on the Internet.

PITCH MEETING TECHNIQUES

The tools identified below will help you catch the interest of professional film people to whom you are pitching.

■ **The movie cross:** A common technique is to compare your movie to two commercially successful films: "It's like *Star Wars* meets *Juno*." Or another technique is to compare your movie to a single movie, as in "This is *The Godfather* but in another business."

■ **The "what if":** What if the latest computer virus is transmitted by email, and you could be infected every time you touch your mouse? This technique allows you to set up an improbable scenario.

■ **The question:** "Have you ever been in love?" Asking the right question personalizes your story to the person you are pitching and makes it more accessible.

■ **Describe the opening shot:** "Do you see the park? Did you notice the park bench? And the bomb underneath it? It's ticking. I am trying to get the big picture, the middle picture, and then the close-up."

Finding script buyers

1 Look at the credits of your favorite films—the production company is always listed.

2 Search for the production company on the Internet or look at www.imdb.com.

3 Read the trade papers, such as *Variety* or *Hollywood Reporter*, for news of film companies.

4 Look for contact details for the producers of films that you enjoy and admire.

5 Send a query letter (see opposite page).

Ongoing research

The trade papers all have websites and publish a free daily headline service. Find and subscribe to at least one of them.

Doing your homework

Choose three different people whom you would like to meet. Research them on the Internet in order to get enough material for discussion in the schmooze.

Write a query letter

Write a succinct letter. Address it to the person you would like to read your script or see your film. But don't send it. You have to write the script first!

Baiting the hook

See if you can summarize your project on one page, including your vision for the project, the budget, the production process, and the story.

Producing &Directing

The producer is the person who makes it all happen. The producer makes the budget, finds the money, hires a director, and supervises the entire process from script to screen. A producer handles all of the commercial questions about the making and marketing of a movie.

The relationship between director and producer is an important one. The director is responsible for everything you see and hear on the screen, and has complete artistic license. The producer fights the commercial battles and must be sensitive to the director's artistic vision. This section takes you through the process of producing and directing.

The budget

A film budget is a spreadsheet that lists everything needed for the film together with an estimate of its cost. A producer's primary concern is deciding which budget fits the film. There are six main types of budget.

1 Hollywood blockbuster budget ($185,000,000–$220,000,000)

Every year or two, Hollywood moguls create the most expensive film ever made, knowing that when it is marketed movie goers will flock to the theaters to see what $150 or $200 million looks like on the big screen. These big blockbusters are described as between $185 and $220 million as though the moguls can't remember what happened to $30,000,000. This is because they are promoting the marketing budget, not the production budget. The first blockbuster film was *Gone with the Wind* and the first million-dollar film was *Cleopatra* with Richard Burton and Elizabeth Taylor.

2 Typical Hollywood budget ($40,000,000–$80,000,000)

This is the approximate total of a typical Hollywood film with one big star. It includes the cost of actually making the film, plus the cost of marketing and advertising the film in North America.

Remember *The Cable Guy*? Jim Carrey was paid about $20,000,000. Paying everyone else to do the movie cost another $2,000,000–$3,000,000. And marketing the film in North America cost about $20,000,000. When asked about the budget of this film, the producers said it was between $40 and $45 million.

3 Low budget ($5,000,000–$10,000,000)

Usually this type of budget is given to directors who have made an interesting and commercially successful film on an even lower budget. The stars are generally from TV and attempting to cross over into movies. These low-budget movies are nicknamed Indiewood, because they are shot to look like independent films, and the storyline and subject matter are generally more risqué than the typical Hollywood budgeted film.

When the Weinstein brothers owned Miramax, they funded many Indiewood films, usually those based on best-selling novels, in the belief that they would be more likely to be nominated for Oscars. And nominated they were, for films such as *The English Patient*, *Cold Mountain*, *Gangs of New York*, *Shakespeare in Love*, *Sicko*, and more than 30 other films.

In Europe a low-budget movie costs under a million. Films at this level are financed by the industry and/or government under the guise of organizations such as the UK Film Council. Such films are subject to labor and union rules, forcing the producers to use relevant unions within their countries. This increases the budget dramatically. Shane Meadow's *This Is England* and James Marsh's *Man on Wire* are industry financed "low budget" films. It is rare to see a filmmaker with an angel investor at this level. Generally the budgets for European films come from government film funds.

4 The million budget ($1,000,000)

Until the early 1990s, this was the entry-level budget. Most new filmmakers debuted with a film of "about a million."

5 Independent micro budget (under half a million)

This is the most common feature film budget in the United States. Armed with half a million and a strong script, a new producer will try to convince an actor with a bit of a name to commit to the film in order to make it easier to sell. Although *Reservoir Dogs* was made for a bit more than half a million—$800,000 in fact—it was called a micro budget feature.

Ultra low-budget moviemaking
By using a limited number of easily accessible locations and keeping the film focused on the characters and their dialogue, in *Reservoir Dogs* Tarantino was able to create a powerful drama on a low budget.

The "digital backlot"
Zack Snyder shot his historical epic *300* on a "digital backlot," a big green screen studio using a handful of real actors in the foreground; the troops and backdrop were created digitally. With a huge budget he was able to do this successfully, and because the film was based on a graphic novel, it was not important for it to look totally realistic.

6 Independent no budget
(under $100,000)

Get a script together, then get a bit of money, and go shoot. This was the route taken by Roberto Rodriguez in *El Mariachi* and Robin Cowie in *The Blair Witch Project*. A generation before, Alfred Hitchcock pulled this off with *Rope*— a modern masterpiece shot over just two days.

The big challenge for films at this budget is to camouflage the production values. There are two strategies here: Shoot until you run out of money, stop for a week or two until you get more, and start up again. This is called "shooting on plastic"; it is the route Christopher Nolan took when he shot *Following* on weekends over nine months. Or, choose a story that benefits from the so-called "shaky camera," like *The Blair Witch Project*.

Make the most of your money

It would be crazy, both logistically and financially, to plan a Cecil B. DeMille-type extravaganza with a cast of thousands of extras for your lo-no budget film. However, with reasonably inexpensive CGI software it is now possible to create such spectacular scenes on a home computer. Of course, if they are not done well then it will be hard for your audience to suspend disbelief.

Rather than spend your limited budget on expensive CGI, why not use your imagination to come up with alternative solutions to the way you tell your story and bring it to screen? It is much better to build a story around what you have available and can afford, especially when you are starting out. *El Mariachi* and *Clerks* are two good examples, as is *Primer*, a low-budget sci-fi time travel movie that relied on great ideas and simple solutions to make it work. Watch these films on DVD, listen to the commentaries, and watch the "making-of" extras to find out how these filmmakers adapted their stories to fit their budgets.

PROJECT 29

Analyze a budget movie

■ Christopher Nolan's *Memento* is an Indiewood film, as is *Donnie Darko*, *The Good Girl*, and *Juno*. Watch any two of these films and write a one-page summary of what you liked and didn't like.

■ These micro-budget films were all commercially successful— *El Mariachi*, *Clerks*, *Pi*, *The Blair Witch Project*. Watch any two of these films and write a one-page summary of each film including what you liked and disliked.

■ Horror can be cheap to shoot. Horror films usually do not have expensive stars, and audiences have learned to accept poor production values if the concept is tight enough. *The Blair Witch Project*, *Reservoir Dogs*, *Night of the Living Dead*, *London to Brighton*, *Once*, *The Brothers McMullen*, and *Following* were mostly made for under $100,000 and all launched huge careers. Watch two of these and write a one-page summary of each film including what you liked and disliked.

The Blair Witch Project
This calling-card feature was shot for about $35,000 on multiple formats and then transferred to 35 mm for its world premiere at the Sundance Film Festival in 1999. The film is an excellent example of a debut low-budget feature.

PROJECT 30

Analyze a million-dollar movie

Each of these movies was made for about a million dollars. Watch the movies, and see if you can decide where the money was spent. Look for expensive location moves, unusual lighting, camera movements, CGI shots, and music and sound effects. Don't worry if you don't get every detail, but you will get a sense of what's possible for a million.

- *Sex, Lies, and Videotape*: $1.2 million

- *Reservoir Dogs*: $800,000

- *Shallow Grave*: $1.9 million

- *Lock, Stock and Two Smoking Barrels*: $1.2 million

- *Blood Simple*: $1.2 million

Million budget (top)
Danny Boyle's directorial debut *Shallow Grave* has all the elements of an excellent million-budget movie: limited locations, strong ensemble cast, a suitcase full of cash, and a gorgeous girl.

Quirky storyline (left)
Quentin Tarantino staked the ground as America's premier director of quirky storylines and on-screen violence with this visually stunning piece. Essentially a stage play, *Reservoir Dogs* has so much emotion and energy it threatens to burst through the theater's walls.

PROJECT 31

Doing it on the cheap

In 1993 a Latino-American filmmaker made a film called *El Mariachi*, which he shot for $7,500. If you haven't seen it, rush out and rent or buy this astonishing feature film by Robert Rodriguez.

On location
Writer/director Robert Rodriguez positioning his actor on location during filming *El Mariachi*. Note the 16 mm camera and the absence of other crew. As sound was added later, no boom operator was needed.

Looking professional

- Much of the battle when trying to raise funds is first impressions, and first impressions start with you. Design your own business card. If you really believe you can make a movie, why not do what professionals do, and call yourself a film producer?

- Come up with a name for your brand new production company. Check on the Internet and in your local company names registry to see if the name is available. Meet with an accountant for advice on how to register the company in order to protect the name and to make certain you comply with local taxation laws.

- Register your company name as a URL to make sure that your company name can have a website. The cost of this can be less than $20. You might want to consider buying different variations on the URL, such as .us, .net, .com, .tv. Each variation will cost between $10 and $75 per year.

MONDAY, NOVEMBER 17
TUESDAY, NOVEMBER 18
WEDNESDAY, NOVEMBER 19
THURSDAY, NOVEMBER 20
FRIDAY, NOVEMBER 21 — Pick up camera!

MONDAY, NOVEMBER 24 — shoot day 3
TUESDAY, NOVEMBER 25 — shoot day 4
WEDNESDAY, NOVEMBER 26 — shoot day 5
THURSDAY, NOVEMBER — shoot day 6
FRIDAY, NOVEMBER 28 — shoot day 7
SATURDAY, NOVEMBER 29 — shoot day 8
SUNDAY, NOVE — shoot day 9 (Last day!) - Return camera tomorr

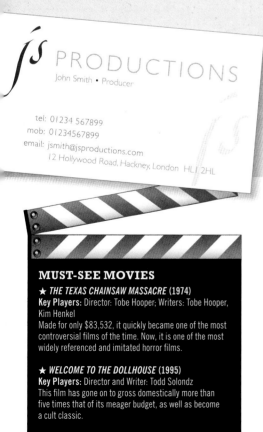

fs PRODUCTIONS
John Smith • Producer

tel: 01234 567899
mob: 01234567899
email: jsmith@jsproductions.com
12 Hollywood Road, Hackney, London HL1 2HL

MUST-SEE MOVIES

★ *THE TEXAS CHAINSAW MASSACRE* (1974)
Key Players: Director: Tobe Hooper; Writers: Tobe Hooper, Kim Henkel
Made for only $83,532, it quickly became one of the most controversial films of the time. Now, it is one of the most widely referenced and imitated horror films.

★ *WELCOME TO THE DOLLHOUSE* (1995)
Key Players: Director and Writer: Todd Solondz
This film has gone on to gross domestically more than five times that of its meager budget, as well as become a cult classic.

Maximizing money spent
Equipment is rented by the week, but priced by the day. Pay for five days (Monday to Friday) but keep for a week. A one-week shoot is nine shooting days. Pick the equipment up on Friday afternoon; return it a week from the following Monday morning. That gives nine shooting days. See if you can negotiate the day rate down. Offer a one-day week, i.e., pay for one day, keep for nine.

Budget lingo
Every industry has its buzzwords. Learning the lingo will help you understand the film industry and present yourself as an insider.

Ninety feet of 35 mm film stock passes through the camera or projector every minute. This means that an 8,100-foot film divided by 90 is 90 minutes long. If you describe the film as a 50,000-foot feature, it means that you have enough money to buy six times the amount of film stock you need—8,100 x 6 is approximately 50,000. In other words, when asked what your budget is, you could say you have a 6:1 shooting ratio, meaning that for every minute of finished film, you have six minutes to play with.

A three-week shoot means 18 shooting days. Only shoot on Sundays if you are behind schedule. A two-week shoot is 16 shooting days as you are shooting every day. A one-week shoot is nine shooting days. Pick the camera up on Friday afternoon and shoot Sat/Sun/Mon/Tues/Wed/Thurs/Fri/Sat/Sun and return the camera on Monday.

Getting organized

Organization is the key to a successful shoot, even if you are doing a simple shoot with a couple of friends at your house.

Learn how to keep track of everything and everyone you are going to need, and make sure they show up at the right place at the right time.

Budgets and schedules are key to organizing the shoot. The budget lists all the things and people you need for the shoot, and the amount of money you are prepared to spend for them. A schedule (see page 57) lists where every thing and every person needs to be in order to get the film made. A production board (see page 40) is a useful organizational device that allows you to see when and where each item and individual is required on the set. The process starts with a script breakdown (see below).

Script breakdown

A script breakdown is the process where everything needed for the shoot is analyzed and listed, ready for the budgeting and scheduling process. Go through your script scene by scene and list every actor, item, prop, and piece of equipment you need to shoot the scene. Another useful reference is to mark the script with different symbols, such as, a circle for wardrobe items, an asterisk for makeup, and use color coding, for example, red for cast members.

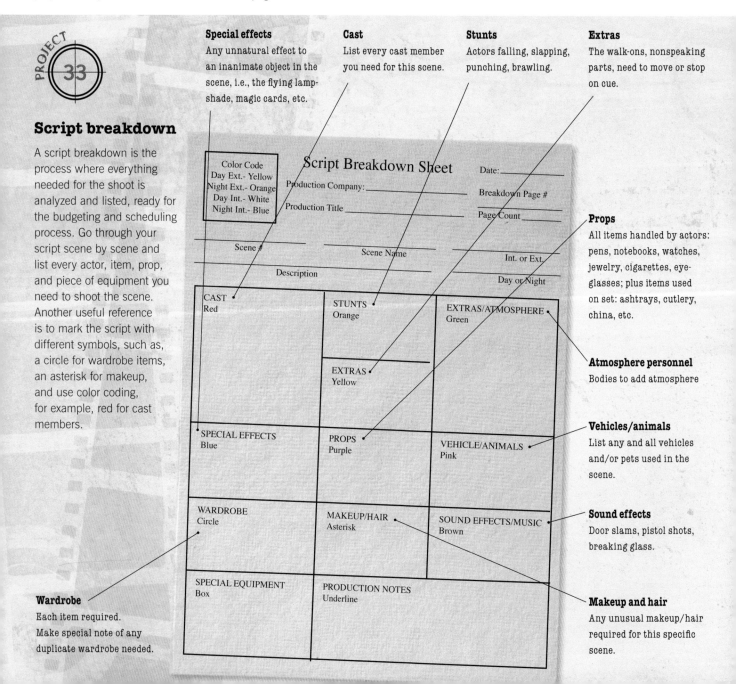

PROJECT 33

Special effects
Any unnatural effect to an inanimate object in the scene, i.e., the flying lamp-shade, magic cards, etc.

Cast
List every cast member you need for this scene.

Stunts
Actors falling, slapping, punching, brawling.

Extras
The walk-ons, nonspeaking parts, need to move or stop on cue.

Props
All items handled by actors: pens, notebooks, watches, jewelry, cigarettes, eye-glasses; plus items used on set: ashtrays, cutlery, china, etc.

Atmosphere personnel
Bodies to add atmosphere

Vehicles/animals
List any and all vehicles and/or pets used in the scene.

Sound effects
Door slams, pistol shots, breaking glass.

Makeup and hair
Any unusual makeup/hair required for this specific scene.

Wardrobe
Each item required. Make special note of any duplicate wardrobe needed.

Script Breakdown Sheet

Color Code
Day Ext.- Yellow
Night Ext.- Orange
Day Int.- White
Night Int.- Blue

Production Company: _____
Production Title _____

Date: _____
Breakdown Page # _____
Page Count _____

Scene # _____
Scene Name _____
Description _____
Int. or Ext. _____
Day or Night _____

| CAST
Red | STUNTS
Orange | EXTRAS/ATMOSPHERE
Green |
| | EXTRAS
Yellow | |
| SPECIAL EFFECTS
Blue | PROPS
Purple | VEHICLE/ANIMALS
Pink |
| WARDROBE
Circle | MAKEUP/HAIR
Asterisk | SOUND EFFECTS/MUSIC
Brown |
| SPECIAL EQUIPMENT
Box | PRODUCTION NOTES
Underline | |

ITEM	DEFERRED	IN KIND	CASH	CREW
ABOVE THE LINE				
Producer			5,000	1
Writer			0	1
Director			0	1
Actors			0	5
BELOW THE LINE				
Film Stock			2,000	
Lab (1)	2,000		0	
Camera			2,000	
Expendables			100	
Sound			500	1
Sound Xfr			800	
Line Producer	2,000		1,000	1
Production Design			0	1
Art Department			500	1
Crew			600	3
Insurance			1,000	
Permits			0	
Location Fees			0	
Art Department/SFX/Stunts			500	
Edge			800	
Office			0	
Food			0	
Publicity			1,500	
TOTAL BELOW THE LINE				
POST-PRODUCTION				
Edit			3–10,000	
Sound Edit			1–2,000	
ADR			1,000	
Foley			1,000	
Music/Score			1,000	
Mix			1,000	
M & E			100	
TOTAL POST-PRODUCTION				
FINISHING				
Titles			1,000	
Cutting/Conforming/Mastering			3–5,000	
Optical Transfer			3,000	
Answer Print				
FINISHING TOTAL				
PRODUCTION TOTAL				
Miscellaneous			0	
Contingency			0	
Legal and accounting	0.25%			
Total Budget				

Above and below the line

Budgets are always divided above/below the line in order to price the talent vs. the technical.

Sound

A key person on the shoot. Find someone with his or her own equipment or access to a cheap rental deal.

Sound transfer

Transferring sound recorded to a format recognized by your computer.

Line producer

Makes sure the film is delivered on time and on budget. The key crew person. Hire someone very organized with a great little black book.

PROJECT

34

Preparing a budget

Using the template, prepare a budget for a $10,000 shoot. List every item, every actor, every crew member, and every location you think you would like to have on the shoot, and then estimate the amount each will cost you. You will need to research costs of hire and purchase for each item, and try to determine what the best price is for each item on your list.

Production board

With the information from the script breakdown sheets, you can now create a production board. This schedule is composed of a backing board and strips of poster board, slotted into place so they can be easily rearranged if necessary.

Production title
Take this from the screen-play.

Scene number
Scenes aren't shot in consecutive order. You might shoot the last scenes first.

End of day 1
The thick black line indicates the end of the day's shoot.

End of day 2

PRODUCTION TITLE: White Angel   PRODUCTION NUMBER: 002

Day/ Night	D	D	D	D	N	N		N	N	D	D		
Internal/ External	I	I	I	E	E	E		I	I	I	I		
Location/ Studio	L	L	L	L	L	L		L	L	L	L		
Scene Number	22	135	136	137	44	93		32	34	65	67		
NOTES: Blue for exterior night; yellow for exterior day; orange for interior night; white for interior day	CONNOR'S BEDROOM	CONNOR'S BEDROOM	HALLWAY OUTSIDE C BEDROOM					BECKY'S KITCHEN	BECKY'S KITCHEN	BECKY'S KITCHEN	BECKY'S KITCHEN		
Breakdown Page Number	99-100		12-13	11	23-25	4		7	9	8	10		
Page Count	1/8	1/8	4/8	2/8	1/8	1/8		1/8	4/8	2/8	2/6		
Timing	00:00	00:00	00:00	00:00	00:00	00:00		00:00	00:00	00:00	00:00		
1- Connor			1	1									
2- Becky			2	2	2			2	2				
3- Joseph										3	3		
4- Elisabeth										4			
Props		1											
Wallet				1									
Gun								1					
Special equipment													
Smoke machine													

Cast (by character name)
List all the characters in the film.

Props
List the main props and the scenes you will need them in.

Choosing and using the camera

The shoot is the fun part where you collect all the images and sounds to be used in the editing room. Selecting the right equipment is vital in determining where and how the finished film will be distributed.

The camera

Cameras can be purchased or rented. Both options have advantages. If you purchase a camera, it is yours, but if it breaks down, you could have a costly repair bill. Renting a camera frees you of maintenance worries and you always get the latest model, but it is inconvenient. A camera takes a series of stills, at a rate of between 24 (film) and 30 (video) frames per second. These stills, when played back, give the impression of movement. The image is captured in a ratio of height to width, depending on what the camera is capable of or what the filmmaker wants.

The image captured by the camera comes into the capture field through a lens. Choosing a selection of lenses enables a cinematographer to "paint" the scene.

Choosing a lens

In 35 mm still or movie cameras, the lower the number, the wider the lens. For example, shooting a restaurant scene with a 12 mm lens would mean that everyone in the entire restaurant would be in frame and in focus. Using a 100 mm lens would mean that the person sitting at the table would be in frame and in focus, but everyone in front of them or behind them would be out of focus.

In 16 mm cameras, the numbers are halved, that is, a 12 mm lens in a 35 mm format would achieve the same results as a 6 mm lens in a 16 mm camera format.

Video cameras

Digital video has become the camera of choice for many new filmmakers. Light and compact, they combine all the features of a film camera, and are easy to use and inexpensive to operate.

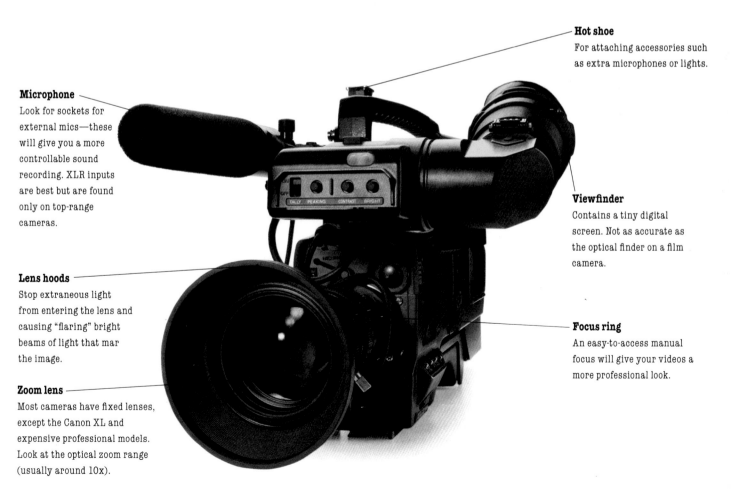

Hot shoe
For attaching accessories such as extra microphones or lights.

Microphone
Look for sockets for external mics—these will give you a more controllable sound recording. XLR inputs are best but are found only on top-range cameras.

Viewfinder
Contains a tiny digital screen. Not as accurate as the optical finder on a film camera.

Lens hoods
Stop extraneous light from entering the lens and causing "flaring" bright beams of light that mar the image.

Focus ring
An easy-to-access manual focus will give your videos a more professional look.

Zoom lens
Most cameras have fixed lenses, except the Canon XL and expensive professional models. Look at the optical zoom range (usually around 10x).

Camera movement

One of the simplest ways to add production values to your film is to move the camera. The industry uses dollies and tracks, such as the low-budget version shown here. When the camera moves through a scene in a big-budget film, it is usually with the aid of a patented and very expensive device called a Steadicam. Low-budget methods include wheelchairs, skateboards, handheld, and Fig Rigs (designed by film director Mike Figgis).

Playing with focus

Use a camera with a manual focus lens and experiment with the effects of using different focal lengths. This can be done with a zoom lens in a fixed position and doesn't have to be a prime (fixed focal length) lens. Find a quiet street or somewhere with a defined background. Put the camera on a tripod and have someone walk toward you, keeping him in focus as he approaches. This is called follow focus. A wide-angle lens (short focal length) will make the background

Choose your format: film or tape?

PROJECT 37

Your first decision will be the medium you capture the pictures on: film or tape. Both formats have pros and cons. Complete the following chart. Organize the cameras and formats first by cost, then by aesthetics. Now choose the appropriate format and camera for your next shoot.

	PROS	CONS
FILM		
35 mm	Superb quality	Expensive
16 mm	Very good quality	Expensive, cheaper than 35 mm
8 mm (entry level format)	Quite cheap	Grainy
DIGITAL FORMATS		
Cell phones (entry-level format)	Cheap and portable	Low res
Mini DV (entry-level format)	Inexpensive	
HDV	Excellent quality	Expensive, but cheaper than 16 mm
HD	Superb quality	Expensive

Camera checklist

PROJECT 38

Draw up a camera checklist. Include all of the items you want or think you need. An example is given below.

CAMERA CHECKLIST
- Lenses
- Tripods
- Batteries
- Cable
- Magazines (if shooting on film)
- Tape or memory sticks (if shooting digitally)

Who's who: camera crew

■ Director of Photography (DoP)
Decides where to place the camera and the lights.

■ Camera Operator
Technician. He or she makes sure everything that the DoP and the Director want is in the frame.

■ Focus Puller
Makes sure that everything is in the frame and in focus. The focus puller measures the distance from the camera to the middle of the eye of the actor, checks to see which type of lens is on the camera, consults a table chart, and then moves the focus wheel until the subject is in focus. On digital shoots, the Focus Puller is called the Imaging Technician. He makes sure that the scenes are recorded and downloaded.

A "focus pull" is the shot where she is full frame and in focus, and he is behind her and out of focus. Then the focus changes, bringing him into focus and she is out of focus. The speed of the focus pull is decided by the DoP and the Director, and is controlled by a dial on the side of the camera.

■ The clapper loader
Is the hardest working person on the crew. This person maintains the camera, loads and unloads the camera, handles the clapperboard, and sends the film to the lab with a camera report.

seem further away but will keep it in focus as the person approaches (1–3). A longer lens will make the background seem closer, and as the person approaches the background will become more out of focus (4–10). This is known as depth of field, which can also be controlled by adjusting the aperture setting (f-stop) on the lens. Long lenses are generally used to isolate the person from the background.

Lighting

Light is the most important tool available to you for enhancing the atmosphere and mystery of your story on camera. On the shoot, you will spend the greater part of your time getting the lighting set up to best represent the scene's aesthetic and emotional impact.

When you look at an actor in front of a wall, you can judge whether he or she is near or far from the back wall. This is because you have two eyes. A camera, however, has just one eye.

Standard lighting

To push the actor off the back wall, filmmakers put a light, called the backlight, behind the actor and shine it on the back of his or her head. You will notice a blue or green halo around actors' heads in big-budget movies. This halo is caused by the backlight.

The actor is now pushed off the back wall, but his face is in shadow. To remove the shadow, filmmakers put a light in front of the actor, called the fill light. Now all the shadows on the face are gone, including the shadows that give a face definition—in the eye sockets and under the nose, lips, and chin. In order to put those shadows back into the face a filmmaker puts a third light, called the key light, in front of the actor. These three lights are arranged until the director and DoP are satisfied. This setup is called three-point lighting. Sometimes, a fourth light is added. It is focused straight into the actor's eyes using a "snoot," which looks like a funnel. This light is called the pick light, and is what makes the actor's eyes sparkle on screen.

Shooting with lights can be time-consuming, as the lights may have to be repositioned a number of times.

Shooting without lights

The French director Eric Rohmer astounded the film industry when he started making films without lights. Thus was coined the phrase, "it was shot with available light."

As the phrase implies, it means using whatever light is available, day or night, inside or out. Modern film stocks and the latest digital cameras are designed to shoot in very low light levels. Scenes shot indoors in a totally dark room, lit by a single candle, can still produce images with exposure and details.

There are pros and cons to shooting without lights. The disadvantage is that you do not control the lighting situations, especially when outdoors or filming near a skylight. The advantages are ease and speed of movement. You do not need to worry about whether or not a camera movement will affect the lighting but can easily move the camera around the set and decide yourself whether or not the lighting is suitable. By using a reflector, even one made from a piece of paper or poster board, you can change and control the light. Look for a consistent, natural light source, such as a spotlight or a sunbeam, and position your reflector so it catches the actor. You can even change the color of the light by changing the color of the paper or poster board.

Three-point lighting

1 The key light
The main light is usually the strongest and has the most influence on the look of the scene. Placed to one side of the camera/subject so that this side is well lit and the other side has shadow.

2 The fill light
The secondary light, placed on the opposite side of the key light. Use it to fill the shadows created by the key. The fill will usually be softer and less bright than the key. To achieve this, you could move the light farther away.

3 The back light
Placed behind the subject to light it from the rear. Rather than providing direct lighting (like the key and fill), its purpose is to provide definition and subtle highlights around the outlines.

Study the masters

Study the paintings of Old Masters to see how they handled light sources and composition. How do these painters handle light and dark? Think about how you would use lighting to illuminate a similar scene.

Spotlight on female figure

Key light on central figures

Camera   Side light illuminating faces in background

Light from a doorway

Light shining through doorway is used as a spotlight effect in Rembrandt's *The Nightwatch*. While it may have been contrived by the artist, it serves to highlight the central characters in the scene.

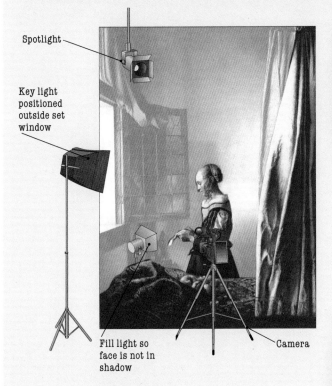

Spotlight

Key light positioned outside set window

Fill light so face is not in shadow

Camera

Window light

In *Girl at a Window Reading a Letter*, Vermeer uses sunlight coming through the window to illuminate the scene. The light and shadows on the wall help to make the subject stand out from the background.

Improvising reflectors

For this exercise you will need three large pieces of construction paper: one white, one beige or cream, and one colored. A goose-necked lamp is useful, and you will also need a friend and a room.

1 See where the light source is coming from. It could be a window or a light fixture.
2 Study the subject's face and see if it is in shadow. If it is, ask him to move so the light source hits him in the eye.
3 Hold a piece of the construction paper under his face to see the reflection. You can change the color with the color of the paper.
4 Finally, plug in the lamp and angle it so it fills in the background. Usually it's best to bounce it off the ceiling. But you decide what you think looks right to you.
5 Make sketches of how you have set up the shot, and make notes of which setup looked best.

Natural light

Natural light, changed by blue reflector

Natural light, changed by red reflector

Experiments with lighting
Keep a record of your findings using a stills camera; label the results.

Work in natural light

Take a stills camera and practice shooting stills using available light inside at home or at work. See if you can change the light by using a simple reflector like a piece of paper or poster board to redirect it. Measure how little light your camera needs to get exposure and detail. Even outdoor work can benefit from reflectors. When outside, notice how you will lose facial expressions, especially if the sunlight is casting strong shadows. A reflector or piece of white poster board held to reflect the sun will bounce the light and detail into the shadow area of the face.

Reflectors
Professional collapsible reflectors can be expensive. A large sheet of white or colored poster board from an art store will also do the job.

Shoot notebook
Use snapshots to remind you of what you've seen.

Basic kit

The phrase "I shot it with a blonde and a couple of redheads" means lights, not people. A blonde is a 1–2,000W lamp and a redhead is a 500–650W lamp. Three of these lights can be packed, with their stands, into a gym bag, transported, and plugged into household electrical circuits.

A useful addition is a range of practical light bulbs—available for a few dollars each. "Practicals" are bought from photographic supply stores. Tell the clerk what you are shooting and the clerk can give you the right bulb, which will screw into domestic light fittings and will help

make your images look great. Photo stores also sell inexpensive portable reflectors, which fold up into small zip bags.

Light show
The shape of the light from a blonde (left) and redhead (right) are changed by altering the position of the barn doors on the light.

PROJECT 42

Keep a shoot notebook

Every time you pass a building or corner of interest, note the way the light reflects down. Note the time, place, and date of any unusual location or light. That way you will start to build up a vocabulary of ideas. An example is shown above.

MUST-SEE MOVIES

★ *SUSPIRIA* (1977)
Key Players: Director: Dario Argento; Writers: Dario Argento and Daria Nicolodi
Low-key, high-contrast lighting, with a mixture of vibrant colors to create a dreamlike atmosphere and enhance the terror.

★ *THE MAN WHO WASN'T THERE* (2001)
Key Players: Directors and Writers: Joel and Ethan Coen; Cinematography: Roger Deakins
Stunning example of well-lit interiors.

Sound

Our brains are wired in such a way that when we struggle to hear sound, the picture dims. The easiest way to make your film look well lit is to make sure the sound is excellent.

Shotgun mic
Has a very narrow recording area, ideal for picking up an actor's voice without background noise. Usually mounted on a boom.

Multidirectional mic
Has a much wider recording area and is generally used to capture ambient sounds.

Wireless with lavelier
These tiny mics and transmitters have to be hidden on the actors without picking up noise from their clothes.

Lavelier
Most commonly used for interviews where it isn't important if they are seen.

Shotgun mic

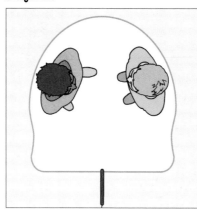

Multidirectional mic

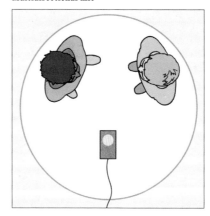

Lavelier mic

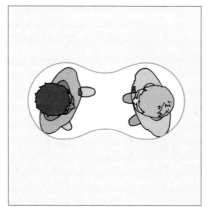

Mic capture patterns
A general indication (above) of the area where each type of microphone picks up sound in relation to the camera.

A sound recordist who can record good, clean sound has become one of the most difficult crewmembers to find. This is ironic since the basics of sound recording can be mastered quite quickly.

A sound recordist's job is to record all of the dialogue and sound effects from the shoot, and to make certain that the sound is delivered to the editor ready for the post-production process.

A good sound recordist knows how to make sure that all of the dialogue recorded in a location sounds as if it was recorded on the same day and in the same room, no matter whether the words spoken were whispered across the room or shouted near the camera.

Sound recording is determined by the quality of the microphone you rent or purchase. Make sure you get the best mic possible for your budget. If you are buying a mic, remember that it can be used over and over again.

A directional or shotgun mic records sound within a narrow radius of where it is pointed. It is used when one actor's voice needs to be singled out. The voice of the actor standing nearby will be barely audible.

A multidirectional mic is used to record all the sound on a set.

A lavelier or clip-on mic is used when an actor may be too far away from the camera, or in an awkward location that makes traditional mics impractical or inconvenient to use. A lavelier is used most commonly on news interviews.

MUST-SEE MOVIES

★ *BARTON FINK* (1991)
Key Players: Directors and Writers: Joel and Ethan Coen
Great soundtrack

★ *PUNCH-DRUNK LOVE* (2002)
Key Players: Director and Writer: Paul Thomas Anderson
Anderson uses abnormally loud noises to create a sense of confusion and nausea, matching that of the main character's emotions on his quest for love.

Recording sound

In a traditional film set, the sound recordist observes how the scene is to be played, consults with the director, who will explain any unusual movements or sound effects, chooses the appropriate microphone, and attaches it to a pole (boom). Sometimes the microphone will be encased in a woolly jacket to cut down on wind noise or other background noise.

When each scene is finished, the director asks everyone to be quiet and the recordist captures a minute of the noise of the room, complete with buzzing lights, rustling costumes, and humming fans. This one-minute recording is called the buzz track, or room noise. The editor will run it underneath any dialogue to make sure it sounds as though it was recorded in the same room.

Special effects like slaps, door slams, breaking glass, and gunshots can be recorded during the shoot, but are often replaced by specialized sounds created in the edit (see page 96).

The sound is recorded on a mixing desk with a good digital record. The master tapes are carefully labeled, and a summary sound report lists the sound for each take. This material is then passed to the editor.

When shooting on video, it makes sense to record the sound directly on camera, providing the sound recordist can hear what is going on. This eliminates the step of synching sound to the picture in edit. Make sure you have a proper XLR (3-pin) sound jack. Don't use the mini plug that comes on your iPod.

Another approach would be to wire each actor with a consumer-quality MP3 recorder, like the iPod, and then record each actor individually using a good quality lavelier mic.

Listen for sounds

Pause and listen for one minute to the ambient sounds in the room where you are right now. List all the different sounds. Note how they build up a texture.

Listen for the buzz track

Take your favorite movie and listen to a favorite scene without watching the pictures. See if you can hear the buzz track or ambient sound.

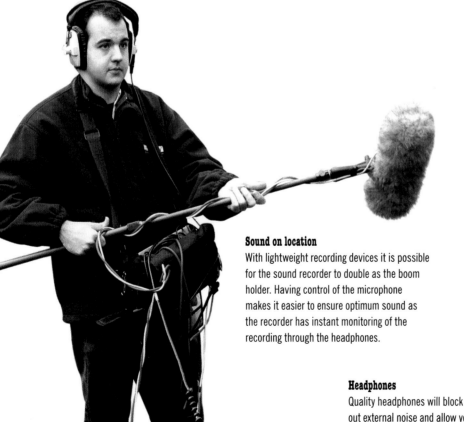

Sound on location
With lightweight recording devices it is possible for the sound recorder to double as the boom holder. Having control of the microphone makes it easier to ensure optimum sound as the recorder has instant monitoring of the recording through the headphones.

Headphones
Quality headphones will block out external noise and allow you to clearly hear a full dynamic range of sounds. Try to match the quality of the headphones with that of your microphone.

The four responsibilities of the director

A director is responsible for directing the screenplay, the actors, the budget, and the camera.

See also
Make a storyboard, page 28
The budget, page 34
How to shoot a movie, page 58

Directing the screenplay

A director's first task is to read and reread the screenplay, looking for the visual details that will help tell the story. The director must then decide what visual details need to be added in order to enhance the story. The director often rewrites the script to incorporate these ideas into a new draft.

PROJECT 45

Come up with visuals

Consider the opening scene of *Reservoir Dogs*. The witty dialogue of the script is complemented by the director's use of the camera as a visual storytelling device. It roams around the restaurant table, weaving the story and providing a close-up of the different characters.

Take this opening description (see above right) and write at least three different visuals about it. For example, you could describe the dishes and cutlery still on the table (see the example, right).

1   INT. UNCLE BOB'S PANCAKE HOUSE—
    MORNING
Eight men dressed in BLACK SUITS, sit around a table at a breakfast cafe. They are MR. WHITE, MR. PINK, MR. BLUE, MR. BLONDE, MR. ORANGE, MR. BROWN, NICE GUY EDDIE CABOT, and the big boss, JOE CABOT. Most are finished eating and are enjoying coffee and conversation. Joe flips through a small address book. Mr. Pink is telling a long and involved story about Madonna.

- The diner is very cheap and dingy.

- The linoleum-covered table is the same sickly yellow as the large, torn, and patched booth they sit in.

- It's not possible to distinguish what they ate, only that it's left big, greasy smears on their plates and silverware.

- The half-filled coffee cups, all with black coffee, don't look much cleaner.

MR. WHITE.
- bald, thin
- mid-thirties

MR. PINK
- short, round-faced
- wears glasses

MR. BLUE
- thick, tall
- black hair
- wears sunglasses indoors

MR. BLONDE
- very thin and gangly
- big eyes

MR. ORANGE
- extremely average looking/
  non-descript

MR. BROWN
- pale skin, bright orange hair
- short and stout

NICE GUY EDDIE CABOT
- Does not look like a nice guy
- A little overweight
- Wears collared shirts

JOE CABOT
- elderly
- bald and stout

PROJECT 46

Cast the scene

Look at the the cast list for *Reservoir Dogs* and decide what sort of actors you would cast if you were directing this scene yourself. It is important to get actors who have the right "look" for the roles (see the example, left).

Rewrite David Lean

PROJECT 47

Read this brief paragraph (below) from *Oliver Twist*, which inspired the movie directed by Oscar-winning director David Lean. Lean's opening sequence for the film is shown in a series of storyboards, below. Reorder these frames and see if you can give the opening a different meaning altogether.

Oliver Twist by Charles Dickens

"Where did she come from?"

"She was brought here last night," replied the older woman, "by the overseer's order. She was found lying in the street. She had walked some distance, for her shoes were worn to pieces; but where she came from, or where she was going to, nobody knows."

A still from Lean's noirish version of the Dickens' classic.

Directing the actors

Screen directing is very different from stage directing. A stage director looks for actors who can develop into the part during the rehearsal process. In film production there is usually little time for rehearsal, so a film director seeks an actor who looks the part, and then won't change.

One of the screen director's many tasks is to find out what the cast can and cannot do, and what they will or will not do. This is done during the audition process.

Finding actors

It's easy to find actors. Everyone, it seems, wants to act. The trick is to find actors suited to the parts in your movie.

Casting on the net

There are websites, for instance shootingpeople.org, that run daily bulletins for actors and filmmakers. Subscribers to the site can display a card outlining their skills, experience, and other personal data. This makes it an excellent starting point, especially as subscribers are already in the lo-no budget mindset.

Another excellent resource is a local theater group or theater workshop. Signing up to take part in actors' workshops is a good way to meet actors, and learning some basic acting skills and techniques will help you as a director. If you understand, firsthand, the acting process, you will be able not only to relate to the talent but also to coax better performances from them. Acting for theater and film are two slightly different disciplines. Film requires short bursts of acting, often understated, that may have to be repeated several times in a short space of time, whereas the stage needs sustained and "large," almost exaggerated, performances. Film acting is more intimate, as you are performing to a very small audience that scrutinizes your every word and movement. Some stage actors have problems adapting to film because they are too theatrical, an approach that appears unnatural on camera. It is therefore very important to have auditions.

PROJECT 48

Placing the casting call

Make a database of local theater groups, acting classes, and amateur dramatic associations. Send them your casting call. Send it to some of your friends as well. Keep track of any interest, and schedule the actors for an audition. Professional film companies send their casting requirements to the three acting guilds for stage, film, and television. These guilds send audition alerts to their members. Another source is Breakdown Services, Ltd, with offices in the U.S. and Canada, which sends news of auditions to agents only. In the United Kingdom, SBS and Professional Casting Report (PCR) perform a similar service. PCR is also available to actors.

Talent on the Web

With a little research, you can find all the talent resources you need. Many websites have links to talented actors looking for work. Some may even consider acting in low- or no-budget productions on which they can cut their teeth.

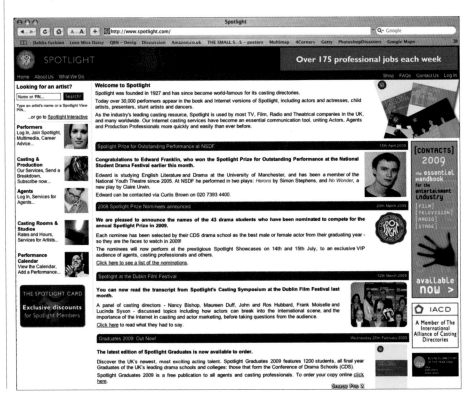

Running an audition

Screen acting auditions consist of a cold reading of two or three pages. Actors attending your audition will be nervous, and the film director's first job is to make them feel at ease and comfortable. Begin by welcoming them. Follow up with some head shots and measurements for the wardrobe department.

When you are both ready to begin, get the actor to read the scene with you or with another actor.

Determining what an actor can or cannot do is quite straightforward. To take a physical example, either she can carry him through the burning coals or she can't. Make sure that any physical abilities or inabilities of your actors are noted during the audition.

When actors have read for the first time, no matter how poorly they have done, praise them on their reading. Remember that they are nervous. Ask them to try it again, but this time give them a direction. Ask them to whisper it, or shout, or read while walking around the room, for example. At this point you will quickly see what an actor will or won't do. Sometimes actors will question your judgment and refuse to follow your direction. This can happen for a variety of reasons. It is usually because of the type of acting they have been taught (and there are many different types of acting theory). Whatever the reason, if the actor refuses to accept your direction, you will not be able to work with him or her. Thank them for their time and move on to the next one.

If at all possible, videotape the auditions. Actors are usually glad that you are making

a visual reference, but it is polite to ask them first.

After you have seen a dozen or so actors for each part, you will start to make a short list. You can call back these actors for a longer audition of, say, half an hour.

Once the audition is over and you have chosen your cast, be very certain that you yourself call each actor back to thank them for their time in attending the audition, even if they were unsuccessful. Actors like to be told whether they haven't got the part—because it means they can move on to the next audition.

On the shoot

People respond differently to situations on the shoot, and actors aren't any different.

Some give their best performance on the first take, some on the third or fourth, and others on the tenth. The skill of a director is managing the cast and getting the best take from the entire cast, whether it be the first, third, or tenth take of a scene.

Prepare a casting call sheet

List all the actors needed for your film. After each character's name write a short, three-line description of the character, making sure you include sex, age range, and any special skills needed, such as horseback riding or swordplay.

After the character description, detail the deal: Whether it is a paid role or not, whether it is for a student or amateur production, approximately when and where the filming is taking place, and how many days the actor will be needed for.

ABIGAIL CHANT
ROLE: the girlfriend, Connie (voice only). She sounds like she is in her twenties.

FEE: Unpaid.

DAYS: 1 day.

LOCATION: Record voice in studio.

Abigail Chant

Directing the camera

Actors will attend your set knowing their lines. When they arrive, the first thing they need to know is where the camera is going to be set up. The director stands where he or she thinks the camera should be placed, and the camera crew starts to build up the camera and lights. During this time, the director rehearses the actors and discusses lens and lighting with the director of photography (DoP). The director then consults with the DoP about which shots to take and in which order.

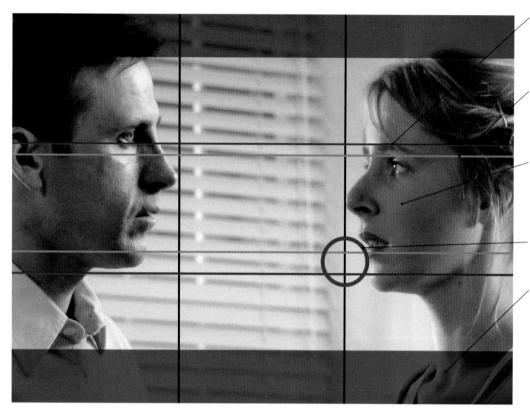

The red horizontal lines show the division for the Academy (4:3) screen version.

The grey horizontal lines show the division for the widescreen (16:9) version.

Notice how the character's facial features remain within the central division in both formats.

Focal point

The gray bands top and bottom show how a letterbox widescreen would look when shot on a 4:3 camera. Because the composition allows for both versions, it is more acceptable to cut off the tops of the heads than to reduce the sides, leaving a large chasm on the screen.

Division of thirds

Dividing your frame into thirds vertically and horizontally is a great aid to composition. You don't need to put the lines on the viewfinder, as approximation is fine.

Identifying beauty

Using a still camera, photograph examples of the Golden Mean in architecture, art, and nature. What gives them their aesthetic appeal? See if a pleasing image follows the Rule of Thirds.

The bridge arches (top right) are in the central division of the frame after dividing the image into thirds horizontally and vertically.

The clouds and buildings (bottom right) are concentrated in the bottom two-thirds of the frame leaving the top almost empty to create a close-knit composition.

Framing the Golden Mean

The most pleasing points of any composition can be calculated from the Golden Mean, which the Ancient Greeks developed. Also called the Golden Section or Golden Ratio, it is a tool to determine the most pleasing point in a composition. An approximate way to find the Golden Mean (or phi as the Greeks called it) is to divide a rectangle into thirds, vertically and horizontally. The points where the lines intersect are called focal or power points.

Crossing the line

When shooting over-the-shoulder shots of two people having a conversation, there is a very specific rule about "not crossing the line." What does this mean? Watch some movies to find examples of how these conversations are shot, and draw a simple diagram to help you understand the principle.

Camera positioning

Follow the camera positions with the images above. Notice how camera position (**3**) "crosses the line," meaning that the actors' positions are reversed on the screen, causing confusion to the viewer.

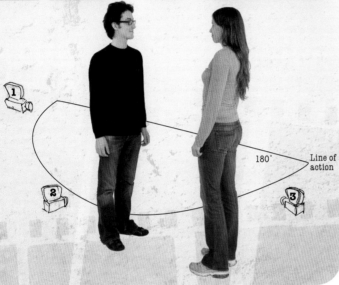

Which format?

The Golden Mean most closely matches the format of modern widescreen HD TVs and video cameras (16:9), but movies have been shot in lots of different formats, such as Academy. Find out the names of all the different formats, their ratios, and the way they can be achieved using both video and film cameras.

Basic shots

Film industry professionals have accepted terms for shot types in order to make communication on the set quick and clear.

- **Master shot:** This shot takes in all the dialogue and any new visual conceived by the director. If the camera is moving at the same time, it is called a fluid master shot.

- **Medium shot (MS):** A shot that is framed from the waist up.

- **Close-up (CU):** A shot of just the face or head.

- **Extreme close-up (ECU):** A shot of just the mouth or the eyes.

- **Cat in the window:** In 1950's American sitcoms, directors favored shots of the family pet turning its head. This gave the editor something to cut to when there was insufficient coverage to cut a scene. Also called cutaway, or B Roll in documentary and news filming.

- **Reaction shots:** Shots of other actors reacting to the dialogue or action off camera.

Repetitive objects (masts, tables, and chairs) and architectural components (arches and towers) are interesting to work with when creating desirable proportions.

The Golden Mean or Rule of Thirds is demonstrated with the shadow and the mountain ridge dividing the frame in a pleasing composition.

Directing at the audition

PROJECT 53

Read this fragment of Tim Clague's BAFTA-nominated short film *Eight* and prepare three different directions for the actors reading for the character of Jonathan.

For example:
- Ask the actor to stand up halfway through the speech; or
- Say it while bouncing a basketball or drinking a beer; or
- Whisper the dialogue.

```
EXT. TERRACED STREET—DAY

Jonathan who is now walking up a long street comprised of semi-
detached and detached houses. He lazily kicks an old can.

                    JONATHAN:
          I know lots of things about my dad I do. He was a
          flower person—I think he grew from a seed.
          (pause)

          And he liked pots....

Dad is seen in fully exaggerated sixties dress, in front of a
floral wallpapered wall, holding a selection of flower pots.

                    JONATHAN(V.O.):
          ...Jesus Lennon...

Dad's hand is pointing at a picture frame. Inside the frame is
a photograph of JOHN LENNON with a halo above him.

                    JONATHAN(V.O.):
          ...and world peas.

Dad is holding a tin labeled "world peas" up next to him in the
style of a 50'S TV advertisement.

EXT. TERRY'S HOUSE—DAY

Jonathan is walking up to the door of the house. He wipes his
nose with his hand and tucks his shirt in. It is a typical
suburban house with a neatly mowed lawn.

                    JONATHAN:
          My dad comes from Liverpool, that's where the sixties
          was y'know.

EXT. PORCH OF TERRY'S HOUSE—DAY

Jonathan and TERRY the same age sitting on the front door step.
Terry now holds the football.

                    JONATHAN:
          This is m' mate Terry.

TERRY just stares unblinking at the camera

                    JONATHAN:
          His dad's nice - I like 'im. He eats 10p crisps and
          supports Man U. We both support England though and we
          watch the match on his telly.

          (pause) (loudly)

          Terry fancies Sophie Huntingdon.

Terry looks even more shocked, snaps out of his camera-induced
trance and starts to speak.
```

Directing the budget

Probably the most important aspect of film directing, from an industry standpoint, is being able to direct the budget. You will already have made a budget (see page 39); now you will have to make a schedule.

Doing the math

Let's suppose you have a 90-page script and a one-week (nine-day) shoot (see page 37). In order to complete the film on time, you need to be able to shoot 10 pages per day. Suppose you have decided that you and your crew can afford to work nine hours per day. This means you have one hour to completely shoot each page of the script (x 10 equals 90 pages). Let's also say that in your budget of tape or film stock you have allowed for 10 minutes for every finished minute. If a page of script is approximately one minute long, then you have 10 minutes of stock for each page (minute) of film. Another way to express this is the shooting ratio. In this case, your ratio is: 10:1. Or, 10 minutes of stock to one minute finished film.

At the end of the day, you want to know how many pages you have shot. You go to the camera operators and find out that they have exposed 100 minutes of stock (10 pages x 10 minutes) and you are on budget. What if the first day ends and you have only shot nine pages? You are behind schedule. This means you will need to add a day to your shoot. What if you overshoot by 10 percent? You are over budget. This means that on day seven you will run out of stock.

At this juncture, you need to take action. If the shoot is behind on the first day, talk to the crew and tell them to speed up, or decide to shoot less coverage. If it is still behind after the second day, talk to everyone on the production and tell them to work faster, or work longer days if they can't keep to the schedule. If they haven't caught up by the third day, then threaten to shut the whole shoot down if they don't catch up, and promise them a big party if they finish on schedule and on budget.

PRODUCTION SCHEDULE V1—*THE THREE PRAYERS OF KITTY JAY*

PLANNING/PRE-PRODUCTION

DATE	TIME	CREW	ACTIVITY	NOTES
MON 26th JAN 2009	10 am	ALL	Pitch Preparation	
TUES 27th JAN 2009	10 am	ALL	Production meeting	
			● Production Schedule run through	
			● Roles & Responsibilities	
			● Script & Scene Disseminate	
			● Crew preparation checklist	
WED 28th JAN 2009	11–12 am	ALL	Production Meeting	
	1–3 pm		● Equipment Lists	
			● Health & Safety	
			● Location Domestic Arrangements	
THURS 29th JAN 2009	10–3 pm		Location Recce	
			● Great Hound Tor Farm	
			● North Bovey	
TUES 3rd FEB 2009 4 pm		ALL	Collect all equipment and items for location shoot / sound recording	
			● Equipment check lists / itinerary	
			● Pack equipment	
			● Props and costumes	
			● Camping & Food	

PRODUCTION

SHOOTING / SOUND RECORDING	TIME	CAST/CREW	SCENE	NOTES
Wed 4th Feb 2009	8 am DEPART	A. BUCKLEY / P. BRUEN	INT/EXT GREAT HOUND TOR FARM	
		CAST—LILI JOHNSON	● Arrival at the farm	
		DRESSER—	● Soap Scene	
		CAMERA—	● Farm Montage	
		CAMERA ASSISTANT—	● Scroll EXT/INT	
		TRACK/DOLLY/CRANE—	● The Reveal	
		SOUND RECORDIST—	● Journey to Church	
		BOOM—	● Lost Cross	
		LIGHTING—	● Symbolic Montage	
		ONLINE EDITOR–	● Pregnancy Reveal	
		PHOTOGRAPHER—	● Leaving Farm	
Fri 6th Feb 2009	3 pm RETURN	DOCUMENTOR—	● Final Scene	

POST PRODUCTION

EDITING		CREW	LOCATION	
W/C 16th Feb 2009 (TBC)		A. BUCKLEY / P. BRUEN		
		EDITOR—B. SHERMAN		
SOUND		CREW—	LOCATION	
W/C 16th Feb 2009 (TBC)		A. BUCKLEY / P. BRUEN		
		EDITOR—B. SHERMAN		
		SOUND RECORDIST—		

FINAL FILM DEADLINE – FRIDAY 27TH MARCH 2009

Make a production schedule

Take the production board on page 40 and analyze what elements are needed at the same time. Use a spreadsheet (detail shown above). List the shoot days, the crew, and cast, then the scenes to be shot. From the production board you will see that an actor might be needed on the first, third, and fifth day. Continue through the entire shooting and editing process until the final date when you plan to complete the film.

How to shoot a movie

How you shoot the movie depends on your script. Is it an action adventure in which characters are constantly on the move? Or is it a drama that all takes place within the confines of a house?

See also:
Choosing and using the camera, page 41
Grammar of film directing, page 60

More often than not, you will need to keep the camera steady, whether it is on a tripod, a jib, or a steadicam. You want the shooting to be as smooth as possible, so the viewers feel as if they are simply watching the events rather than a "movie." Nothing shouts "amateur" more than an unsteady camera. However, there can sometimes be a reason to include a "shaky camera" as an effect. A recent trend in horror movies, which is quickly becoming overused, is to have the camera point of view as one of the characters. In *Cloverfield* this effect is achieved with video camera footage. In *Quarantine* the premise is that a news crew is shooting the events unfolding.

Then there is the lighting. Generally, your characters should be brighter than the background. The viewers need to be able to see the characters and what they are doing. For indoor shoots you will probably need lights. For daytime, outdoor scenes you might not need any lights, though you might need lighting equipment, such as reflectors to redirect sunlight. Of course, the lighting also determines the mood of a scene and a film so your lighting has to fit with what your script conveys.

The various shots that make up a scene need to be well framed. This also determines the composition of a scene. If two characters robbing a bank are talking about cracking the safe, then your shot will include both of them and the safe. You do not want to have one of the characters cut off in the picture, as it will be too distracting.

Also, it's a must that you get adequate coverage of a scene. The best way to think about this is to envision how it will go together in editing. Will the scene cut together if you are using a wide shot, medium shot, or close-ups? Or perhaps the entire scene is in a wide shot and you know, according to the script, that you

PROJECT 54

Breaking a movie down into shots

Watch a scene in a movie and write down the different shots used (wide/medium/close-ups) and why you think they used those shots in that order. A sequence from *Elf* (2003) is analyzed here.

In this scene, the father (James Caan) is walking down a busy New York City street when he sees his son, Buddy, sleeping in a department store window.

1 **Moving wide shot** as father walks toward the camera and down the street, a man in his own world. The shot stays wide and follows him to when he stops and looks in the department store window.

4 **Medium shot** of father looking at Buddy in window widens out to wide shot when Buddy wakes up. The wide shot distances him from his son.

5 **Medium shot** of father staring through the window.

Your shooting crew

A minimal crew would be made of, from left to right: Assistant Director (AD), to keep everything running smoothly; director of photographer (DoP)/cameraman; focus puller; clapper loader/continuity; sound recordist/boom op. It is possible to shoot with fewer people—or, of course, more.

won't need any of the other shots. Director Jim Jarmusch's early films rely on this use of wide shots. On a low-budget movie, you may only have a 3:1 ratio, meaning you shoot three times as much footage as you'll be using. On a Hollywood movie this could be a 10:1 ratio, or even higher.

Lastly, there are the transitions between the scenes. Keep in mind how the scenes are going to flow together. Does one scene just "cut" to another or does it fade down to black and then fade back up to the next scene? This also, in part, will determine how the movie is shot.

2 **Medium shot** of father's reaction, frowning, as he gazes through the window at the man asleep.

3 **Close-up** of the sleeping Buddy's face. This shows that the father is focused on his son.

6 **Wide shot** as Buddy's hand reaches out in the foreground to touch the glass, a small crowd watches. Buddy wants to connect with his father.

7 **Wide shot** as Caan's character quickly walks away. He's quickly distanced himself from the situation.

Grammar of film directing

In order for a director to be able to communicate effectively with the entire crew, the film industry has developed a series of terms that describe basic techniques. Successful directors understand these terms and use them appropriately.

See also:
Choosing and using a camera, page 41
Editing, page 92

The relationship between the camera and the actors is one of the most expressive creative tools available to a filmmaker. The placement of the camera alters the relationship between actor and viewer. It can shape the viewer's perspective of shape and time. Camera height, angle, distance from the actor, composition and framing, long takes, short takes, and the way a camera moves in and out of a scene, following or tracking characters, are all elements a filmmaker needs to understand and exploit to advantage.

Camera shorthand

Films and movies have a unique language to express how the camera is moved and used. The basic shots and techniques of directing and camera movement were established in the 1920s. However, the means of moving the camera and the mechanics of cameras themselves have continued to evolve.

Panning: The camera moves from side to side, from high to low, or low to high.

Tracking shot: In this technique, the camera is placed on track and moves alongside an object or actor in motion.

Crane shot: A camera is attached to a device that can swing and tilt the camera high above the actor's head. The crane can move the camera up and down, toward, or away from the actor.

Zoom: The lens of the camera is adjusted to make objects move closer to or further away from the camera.

PROJECT 55

Camera angles

For this you will need an actor and a camera. Try taking shots from each of the following angles:

Level camera angle
A camera angle that is even with the subject. It's considered a neutral shot.

High camera angle
A camera angle that looks down on its subject. It's considered to make the actor look small and weak. This shot was taken from a stepladder.

Steadying the camera

Watch a scene in a movie and write down what you think they used to steady the camera (if anything) and what effect this has. The examples on the right, are from the scene in *Get Smart* (2008) that first introduces the film's villain, Siegfried.

1 Dolly and steadicam: The first shot has the camera on a dolly or steadicam so it's a very smooth movement. It starts low to the ground and first goes past a military-type truck to reveal a sinister-looking warehouse. The low angle makes the building seem huge and so intimidating.

2 Moving shot: There is another moving shot inside the warehouse, which shows two men looking for something. The shot matches the outside and reveals the two characters, who seem small inside of the big building.

3 Static, tripod shot: Then a static, tripod shot of the two characters as they find what they are looking for, so we can register who these guys are as we see them later in the movie. There's a smooth tracking or steadicam shot as the camera moves from a wide shot to a close-up of a shadowy figure, who is the villain. The movement of the camera focuses on him, which gives him a sense of power.

4 Smooth tracking or steadicam shot: As the camera moves from a wide shot to a close-up of a shadowy figure, who is the villain, the director uses a smooth tracking or steadicam shot. The movement of the camera focusing on the villain gives him a sense of power.

Identify shot types

Study the shot type in column 1 and try to match up the shots with the elements of a story in column 2 (see page 94 for more information).

Column 1:
1 Extreme long shot
2 Master shot
3 Medium shot
4 Close-up
5 Extreme close-up
6 Point of view
8 Low camera angle
9 Tracking shot

Column 2:
a They walk down the street.
b She listens intently.
c He takes a sip of coffee.
d A tear wells in her eye.
e He rides off into the sunset.
f She chases after her son.
g Conveyor belt sushi
h Towering over followers

Camera transitions

A movie is made up of a series of shots. Each shot is made from a different angle and then joined together by the editor in a transition. Watch a movie and see if you can spot at least three different transitions (see page 93).

Adapting camera moves

Study the camera movements listed below and describe how they might be used in your story.

Low camera angle
A camera angle that looks up at its subject. It's considered to make the actor look powerful. Try lying on the floor with your camera pointing up at the actor as they walk over you.

POV (point-of-view) shot
A shot that is seen from the point of view of a character within the scene. Pretend that you are the main character. Point the camera in front of you, so we can see what you (the main character) see.

Reaction shot
The shot of a person reacting to another actor's lines. Get an actor to look into the camera and react to lines of dialogue that you read out.

Trick shots

A camera provides a wide range of functions that offer a filmmaker a variety of techniques. This can enhance the production value of a movie.

See also
Make a storyboard, page 28
Editing, page 92

A filmmaker's challenge is to tell stories using the powerful cinematic tools offered by the camera. The reality we know in daily life can be manipulated and changed for dramatic effect.

The camera's functions and the nature of filmmaking offer many possibilities that can enhance the production value of your film. Using these functions allows filmmakers to create realistic-looking special effects.

Combining your camera's trick shot functions with these techniques will make you look like an experienced filmmaker, and your film like a professional production.

Some of these techniques happen in-camera; some are a combination of in-camera shooting with post-production editing techniques.

Using blue screen
Spartan epic *300* (main picture and inset) was shot entirely on a digital backlot, a large blue-screen studio space where the background is added digitally afterward.

PROJECT 60

Green screen/blue screen effects

If you are working on a really low budget but want the big budget look, why not consider blue or green screen? Shooting green screen means that you can layer the actors over any type of background you want—from the Himalayas to a space ship.

Get a large green or blue sheet (alternatively, paint a wall) and light it as brightly as you can. Place your actors as far as possible from the screen. Make sure that they are not wearing anything close to the color of the background (or else that part of them will disappear too!) Light your actors to look as much as possible like the scene you are going to put them in. When it comes to editing on a program like iMovie, import the clip of the actors as well as the background. Select "blue screen smooth" on the foreground clip and play back. You may have to use the blurring tool to round out any bright edges.
Sample clip: *300*

PROJECT 61

Day for night

Take your camera outside in the daytime. Change the light settings to manual. You can then adjust the settings until the scene goes very dark or nightlike. Try to keep several light puddles to avoid an overall grayness. You can also scroll through the White Balance and adjust your camera for color effects.
Sample clip: *28 Days Later*

PROJECT 62

Ghosting

This is the poor man's green screen and is easy to do. Shoot the first scene with as much dark or black as possible on one side of the frame. Then shoot the second image to be "ghosted" leaving black but on the other side. Dark or nighttime scenes work best. When you are finished, drop the main shot on track one, and the layered image on track two.

Sample clip: *Close Encounters of the Third Kind*

PROJECT 63

Moving objects

Here's how to make an object fly across the room: Have your actor throw an object into the frame. Played in reverse, it looks as though the object rose off the floor and headed straight toward the actor. In *Harry Potter and the Order of the Phoenix*, nylon line was tied to an object, which was then tugged out of Harry's hand. That way, his hand doesn't move and it looks as if the object flies straight into his palm.

Sample clip: *Harry Potter and the Order of the Phoenix*

PROJECT 64

Budget lighting effects

Stylized lighting can create mood and atmosphere. Try these ideas:

- Aim a bright light at a tray of water. Make the water ripple so that you see the reflections from the light on your set.
- Make cardboard cutouts (called gobos) and place them in front of your lights to create patterns to resemble prison bars, snowflakes, or street signs.

Sample clip: *Bladerunner*

Slo-mo foregrounds

Rehearse your actor in a scene in which she moves at a consistently slow rate—a bit like a mime artist. Photograph a background at normal speed but from a locked tripod that won't move. When the two images are laid on top of each other with a speed filter applied, your actor will appear to be walking in a dreamlike trance.

Sample clip: *Trainspotting*

Walking backward

Have your actor walk backward through a crowded street. When played in reverse it will look like the crowd is walking backward while your actor is walking forward. This will take practice to avoid crashing into parking meters and other pedestrians. Try to get a long, uncut shot for maximum effect.

Sample clip: *The Time Machine*

Slo-mo backgrounds

Rehearse and shoot a scene at double time against a moving background. When slowed down to normal speed, the scene will still look as though the background is moving very fast. The audio (if any) will have to be re-recorded in ADR.

Sample clip: *Fear and Loathing in Las Vegas*

Forced perspective

PROJECT 68

You can cheat the way an actor looks in relation to the background by placing him at certain angles to the camera. To shrink actors, place them farther from the camera. To make them look larger, bring them closer to the camera. You can also make models of objects that are larger or smaller than reality to make your actors look larger or smaller. Or use green screen techniques to place them into another background.

Sample clip: *Lord of the Rings* (the hobbits were shot like this in order to give them a background to react to).

Duplicating an actor

PROJECT 69

This lets you show an actor with his double in the same scene. You will need edit software with a linear wipe function (such as Adobe Premiere) that allows you to make half of the frame transparent. Shoot the scene with the camera locked on a tripod, with the lighting and focus set to manual, with the actor on one side of the screen. Don't let the actor cross the center line from left to right. Then shoot the second scene with the actor on the other side of the screen. Layer one clip above the other in the edit timeline. Drag the transparency filter onto the first clip, adjust the settings, and blur the edges. Repeat for the other side.

Sample clip: *Multiplicity*

One ring to rule them all...
Forced perspective and digital trickery were used to make Elijah Wood's Frodo appear diminutive next to Ian McKellen's imposing Gandalf in Peter Jackson's *Lord of the Rings*.

Seeing double and then some
Multiple takes and post-production techniques meant that Michael Keaton could share screen time with himself in Harold Ramis' *Multiplicity*.

Shooting on location

Shooting on location implies shooting on private property, or on public property like parks and streets. Rules apply. Make sure you understand them.

A great way to enhance production values is to choose a great-looking location—one that is filled with mood and atmosphere that would take a lot of money to recreate in a studio.

There are different rules for shooting on publicly owned or privately owned property.

Shooting on private property

To shoot on private property, you will need to apply directly to the property owner. If you want to shoot in an apartment, you will also need to apply to other relevant parties, such as Housing Associations or Residents' Committees.

It is recommended that you get a location release form signed by the owner of anywhere you shoot. The release form outlines the days and hours you can access the property, allows you legal permission to use the location, and determines the location fee (if any). In case of a dispute, the release form can be used to remind everyone of the agreement

Guerilla filmmaking

One of the meanings of the phrase "guerilla" filmmaking is shooting without

Location release form
This is an example of the contract you should sign when using someone's private property.

Property address
List the address of the property you are using.

Compensation
Write in words and figures the money you have agreed to pay.

LOCATION RELEASE FORM

Having full authority to do so, I hereby grant (name of production company, or, filmmaker's name) _____ permission to use the property at (address of property) _____ for the purposes of photographing and recording scenes for the production (production name) _____ during the hours of (access time to wrap time) _____ on the following days: (name and date each day you plan to shoot)

Permission includes, but is not limited to, the right to bring cast, crew, equipment, props, and temporary sets onto the premises for the time specified.

Total compensation for the specified time period will be: _____ (state a numeric value, even if it is $1.00) for which the undersigned acknowledges receipt.

I understand that all items brought onto the premises will be removed at the end of the production period and that the location, including buildings, landscaping, and all things associated with same will be fully returned to their original condition, except as mutually agreed upon and indicated below:

(List items that may not need to be redecorated. If rooms need to be redecorated, specify the paint type and product number.)

_____
_____

It is further understood that any damage to the property will become the responsibility of the production company and any needed repair or restoration will be carried out within 14 days of the last specified day of production.

Production company _____
Signature _____ Printed name _____
Title or position in company _____
Address _____
Phone number _____ Date _____
Property agent (or owner) _____
Signature _____ Printed name _____
Title _____
Address _____
Phone number _____ Date _____

Production company
Write your company's name. You are undertaking to compensate the property owner for loss and damage.

Telephone number
Include daytime and nighttime contact numbers.

Address
List the address you are trading from.

Sample release form
This doesn't constitute a proper legal document, but it illustrates the key clauses that you would want to consider including.

PROJECT 70

The paperwork

Study the sample location release form and the suggested format for a group release form given on page 68. However, remember that these forms are not proper legal contracts. If you want to use one, you will need to consult a lawyer who is versed in this aspect of the law and can advise you about drawing up a form that will cover the specific details of your location and shoot.

permits or permissions. This is called "stealing the shot." Most local laws state that a permit is necessary when shooting with a tripod. Obviously, then, shooting handheld exploits this loophole. Try to explain that to an irate police officer, however, and you run the danger of having your equipment impounded.

Shooting on public property

It is recommended that you get an official permit every time you shoot in a publicly owned park, street, or pavement.

Permits are granted by local municipal government offices, or by local film commissions. You will be asked to complete an application form detailing what you are shooting and when. Your application will be assessed and you will normally be asked to pay a fee to cover the cost of hiring extra police officers to supervise your shoot and make sure traffic is not impeded and that health and safety rules are obeyed. Sometimes you will be asked to pay the amount of money lost from parking meters being out of use as well.

Certain public areas are off limits: airports and certain government offices due to anti-terrorist prevention security fears. On top of that, common sense and the law dictate that you should always inform the police if you plan to shoot a scene that includes any violence or weapons, even if it is only a fake gun or sword.

Finding locations

One of the best ways to get a great location is to befriend the owner or management agent who cares for the property. The most common place to start is with home owners. Many films are shot in the homes of the filmmakers (or those of their relatives). Personal contacts might yield abandoned warehouses, disused schools or hospitals, or restaurants.

Certain locations, such as bars, can be used early in the morning until they open for business. Other locations may seem cheap, when in fact they are in awkward locations, which hikes up transport costs.

Another good source of locations are specialized location agencies, which attempt to provide film rental income for their owners, and local film commissions, which know of many hidden locations and can advise on negotiating fees and completing location release forms.

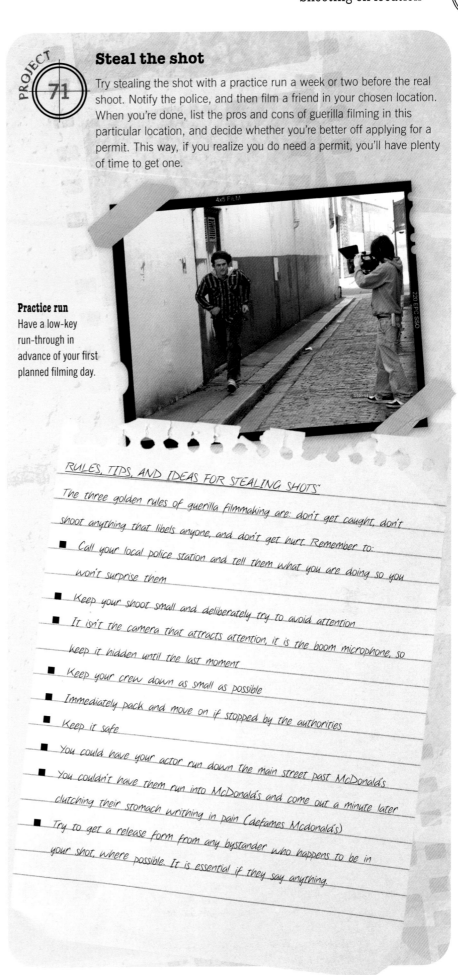

PROJECT 71

Steal the shot

Try stealing the shot with a practice run a week or two before the real shoot. Notify the police, and then film a friend in your chosen location. When you're done, list the pros and cons of guerilla filming in this particular location, and decide whether you're better off applying for a permit. This way, if you realize you do need a permit, you'll have plenty of time to get one.

Practice run
Have a low-key run-through in advance of your first planned filming day.

RULES, TIPS, AND IDEAS FOR STEALING SHOTS

The three golden rules of guerilla filmmaking are: don't get caught, don't shoot anything that libels anyone, and don't get hurt. Remember to:

- Call your local police station and tell them what you are doing so you won't surprise them
- Keep your shoot small and deliberately try to avoid attention
- It isn't the camera that attracts attention, it is the boom microphone, so keep it hidden until the last moment
- Keep your crew down as small as possible
- Immediately pack and move on if stopped by the authorities
- Keep it safe
- You could have your actor run down the main street past McDonald's
- You couldn't have them run into McDonald's and come out a minute later clutching their stomach writhing in pain (defames McDonald's)
- Try to get a release form from any bystander who happens to be in your shot, where possible. It is essential if they say anything.

Group release form

If you are shooting on location, or if you are using a large number of extras, it can be difficult to ensure that everyone has signed a release form. Even if you succeed in tracking down every extra, it could result in a huge file that will be difficult to manage. In such circumstances, it makes sense to use a group release form. Most forms follow a standard format. Look at this one.

GROUP RELEASE

To: Your Production Company Name:

I, the undersigned, hereby grant permission to .... to photograph me and to record my voice, performances, poses, acts, plays and appearances, and use my picture, photograph, silhouette and other reproductions of my physical likeness and sound as part of the ...... tentatively entitled .... (the "Picture") and the unlimited distribution, advertising, promotion, exhibition and exploitation of the Picture by any method or device now known or hereafter devised in which the same may be used, and/or incorporated and/or exhibited and/or exploited.

I agree that I will not assert or maintain against you, your successors, assigns and licensees, any claim, action, suit or demand of any kind or nature whatsoever, including but not limited to, those grounded upon invasion of privacy, rights of publicity or other civil rights, or for any other reason in connection with your authorized use of my physical likeness and sound in the Picture as herein provided. I hereby release you, your successors, assigns and licensees, and each of them, from and against any and all claims, liabilities, demands, actions, causes of action(s), costs and expenses whatsoever, at law or in equity, known or unknown, anticipated or unanticipated, which I ever had, now have, or may, shall or hereafter have by reason, matter, cause or thing arising out of your use as herein provided.

I affirm that neither I, nor anyone acting for me, gave or agreed to give anything of value to any of your employees or any representative of any television station, network or production entity for arranging my appearance on the Picture.

I have read the foregoing and fully understand the meaning and effect thereof and, intending to be legally bound, I have signed this release.

NAME	ADDRESS	SOC. SEC. NUMBER

Your Company name and address

Paragraph 1 introduces the contract. In return for receiving a screen credit the following production company (name) has the right to use their image, likeness, and anything else resulting from their involvement in the production. It states that all of these elements may be used in a specific production (title of the project).

Paragraph 2 makes clear that these rights are permanent and apply to every country in the world and to every stage of the production through to delivery of the finished film and on every format—including film, HD, DVD, and web formats—even if you do not plan to use all of them.

Paragraph 3 confirms no under the table payments or return of favors are expected or received by the extras.

Paragraph 4 is shown as a list. It is best to draw up a grid that gives enough space for each person's full name, signature, address, I.D. and social secuirty number. The list may extend to several pages if there are a large number of people

At the bottom allow a space for your signature and the date.

PROJECT 73

Talent release form

Read over this sample release form, carefully making notes of things that you don't understand completely. Then go back and look over those hazy areas. Do some Internet or library research to help you fully grasp these ideas—it's important to know exactly what you're signing, especially when it concerns the safety of other people.

Ownership

This industry clause means that the production company now owns 100% of your contribution to the film. Make sure you are happy with this before signing.

Liability

You will most likely want to buy your own liability insurance.

Cast and Crew Release

I accept all of the conditions and provisions of the following release form covering my work on the production which is tentatively titled "[name of your film]" and which is being produced by "[name of the production company]."

Ownership

I assign to "[name of the production company]" the ownership and all rights to use, exhibit, distribute, assign, license, and otherwise promote the products of my work on the production. I also waive any and all claims to copyright, patent, or other ownership of my work products on the productions.

I agree to keep confidential all written, creative, technical, and financial detail of the production unless authorized or requested by "[name of the production company]" to disclose such information.

Liability

I indemnify "[name of the production company]," the owners of any locations used, and the owners of any uninsured equipment against any claims and demands of personal injury, damage to property, and death resulting from my work on the production.

I understand that I am responsible for all necessary personal injury, death, and liability insurances, and am responsible for any damage caused by my actions and by my personal property used during my work on the productions. I accept full responsibility for all personal risks during my work on the production.

Compensation

Unless it is otherwise stated in the "Description of and Assignments of Interest of Profits..." Contract, I am volunteering my services for the productions and will receive no monetary compensation. I understand that I will receive credit under the following name in the screen credits of the completed production:

I have read the foregoing release, authorization and agreement, before affixing my signature below and warrant that I fully understand the contents thereof.

Name for Screen Credits:

Signature:

Date:

PROJECT 74

Location log

Researching potential locations is an important task. You never know when you are going to need a certain type of location. Locations can also suggest valuable story lines. A location log should list the following categories on one axis of the form: owner/manager; available hours; location fee (if any); power; windows; site security; access; closest police station; hospital; parking; transportation; special notes; pictures (your visual reference for the location). The other axis should list: Location 1; Location 2; Location 3; etc.

LOCATION LOG: Location 1

OWNER/MANAGER:

AVAILABLE HOURS:

LOCATION FEE:

POWER:

WINDOWS:

SITE SECURITY:

ACCESS:

Risk assessment form

Health and safety issues are all important and your responsibility as a filmmaker is to ensure that every member of your cast and crew works without fear of injury. Here is a sample risk assessment form.

Create a location form

Make your own sample location form and use your location notebook to fill in the details. The form should have a square for the location photograph, a grid for the address and owner's details, time and date, kind of camera used, map, and transportation details.

RISK ASSESSMENT FORM

Activity assessed	Assessment date	Assessed by	
Activity location	Who's at risk	Next assessment before	Approved by
Hazard	Residual risk level* (BEFORE)	Residual risk* level* (AFTER)	Control measures reducing the risk level to an acceptable level
Personal protective equipment needed	Provided by	Level of first aid provision needed	First aiders
Nearest telephone		Nearest 24 hour hospital and/or doctor	

Risk factors are calculated from 1 (neglible) to 5 (very severe). "Residual risk before" means during the original survey of the location.

"Residual risk after" refers to level after safety measures have been put in place.

* Refer to the risk assessment scoring guidelines

SAMPLE LOCATION FORM

Location/Owner	My house
Available hours	Monday–Wednesday, any time
Location fee	None
Power	No more than 2500W lights plugged into any one room. Check fuse box.
Windows	Big front windows in living room but they have shades
Security	Secure
Access	Give people directions via MapQuest, plus e-mail them directions of where to go once they drive through town
Police/Hospital	Within 2 miles
Transportation	Actors will drive themselves to location.

Find out about local regulations

Local government offices usually have a film department that looks after accommodating and licensing film crews. Get in touch with them and find out what laws apply where you are.

The local bylaws will include commonsense regulations regarding cabling, coning, children, firearms, and other basic health and safety issues like night shoots, use of generator, and wet downs (artificial rain). Local governments want to make sure that you do not make a nuisance of yourself, obstruct others from going about their business, cause a disturbance, or cause a hazard.

PROJECT
78

Build a story around a place

Robert Rodriguez launched his career with a film called *El Mariachi*. He came up with the idea by listing all of the locations he had free access to, and built his story around the locations. You can do the same with your locations.

Locations
List of locations
available for free

LOCATION 1:

DIRECTOR'S APARTMENT, NYC
(can double as several apartments
– rearrange the furniture, etc).
AVAILABILITY: Any time.
CONTACT: Self.

LOCATION 2:

EMPTY FLOOR OF BUILDING.
AVAILABILITY: Weekends–just
need to tip freight elevator guy.

LOCATION 3:

CORNER DELI.
AVAILABILITY: Any time–just make sure to
let owner know at least a week beforehand.
CONTACT: Owner.

LOCATION 4:

ACTOR'S APARTMENT, NYC.
AVAILABILITY: After 6pm weekdays, any time weekend.
CONTACT: Actor.

Making stuff look good

Making your shoot look good for the eye of the camera is the job of the production designer. The production designer is hired by the director and creates all the drawings for the sets, wardrobes, and props. The art director realizes the drawings.

See also:
Props and set dressing, page 76
Makeup, page 78
Wardrobe, page 82

The art department is led by the production designer, who collaborates with the director and the director of photography and creates the drawings and plans for the visuals used during the shoot: props, wardrobe, and sets. The execution of these ideas is managed by the art director.

A good production designer adds creative input to the film, in discussion with the director (on creative issues) and the producer (on financial issues). The production designer then oversees the other art department heads: props, wardrobe, makeup, and set building and decoration. A production designer will have a good visual eye and will be able to clearly express her creative vision to the director and the art department team. The best way to do this is by drawing and sketching.

To get a job as a production designer you must learn how to develop visual concepts and how to transform designs into reality on both sound stages and locations using digital imaging software and CAD/CAM software, as well as traditional drawing techniques.

Why build a set?

One of the main reasons for shooting on location is budget. If you have an existing setting then you don't have the expense of building something from scratch. However, shooting on location presents its own set of problems. Budget considerations apart, building a set gives the production designer total control over the look of the scene without having to resort to redecorating someone's house. The biggest advantage comes when shooting, because the set can be built in modules that can be moved to allow cameras to be positioned where the director wants them, and the director of photography can place the lights without obstruction.

Devising such a film set requires the same level of detail as any other architectural design, showing floor plans, elevations (front and side views), as well as three-quarter view sketches with color plans, all of which are given to the construction team. Of course the main difference is in the construction because film sets are only built to last weeks and are then destroyed, so inferior materials and short cuts are often used, and these are outlined on the plans.

Architectural drawings for a set
Designs for a film set (right) often require the same level of technical input as an actual interior.

Popular professional programs

There are a number of fairly affordable, easy to use computer programs that can make your film and promotional documents look sharper and more professional. These include:

■ **Design:** Vectorworks, SketchUp

■ **Graphics:** Adobe Creative Suite (Photoshop, Illustrator)

■ **Photography:** Aperture, Photoshop, Photomatix, Stitcher

■ **Admin:** Excel, Pages, Omnifocus

You should learn these programs if you have a serious interest in working as a production designer or art director.

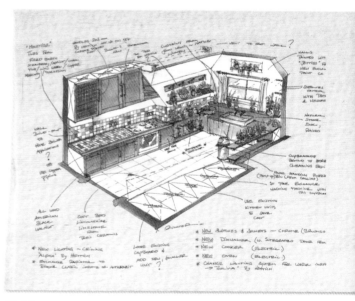

Sketch
A three-quarter view of the set, containing notes from the production designer regarding color schemes and materials to be used.

Practice your drawing

PROJECT 79

Choose a sample scene from a movie and draw an artist's impression of the scene. Try to convey the emotion of the scene. The drawing has to have enough detail to inspire the art director, scenic and wardrobe personnel, and props makers. There's an example shown below.

Artist's impression
Artist's sketches (below) get down on paper stills from scenes from Peter Webber's *Girl with a Pearl Earring* (right).

Who's who
Art Department

■ **Production Designer**
Does drawings for set, props, and wardrobe in consultation with the Director and Heads of Department.

■ **Art Director**
Supervises the execution of the drawings.

■ **Scenic Painters**
Paint sets and carry out touch-ups on shoot.

■ **Scenic Carpenters**
Build sets.

■ **Props Master (see page 76)**
Finds and/or builds props.

■ **Set Dresser (see page 76)**
Sources and arranges props on set.

■ **Wardrobe (see page 82)**
Creates or hires the wardrobe and maintains costumes during shoot.

■ **Makeup (see page 78)**
Creates normal stage makeup and special effects, such as gore.

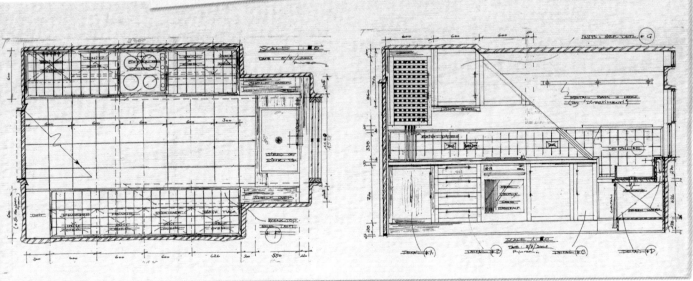

Floor plan
A top view of the set, giving precise measurements for the set builders to follow.

Elevation
The front view of the set, showing measurements and details not seen on the floor plan.

Maquettes

Architectural models are an important part of the production designer's arsenal. Not only do they show how the set looks and works but, if built large enough, they can also be used by the DoP to try out lighting and the director to block scenes.

Maquettes can be built with cardboard although foamcore board (available from good art suppliers) is more commonly used. This material is more durable than cardboard and can be easily cut with a craft knife. Panels can be painted or have photographic textures pasted onto them. The important thing is to follow the designer's plans and drawings so that everything is to scale.

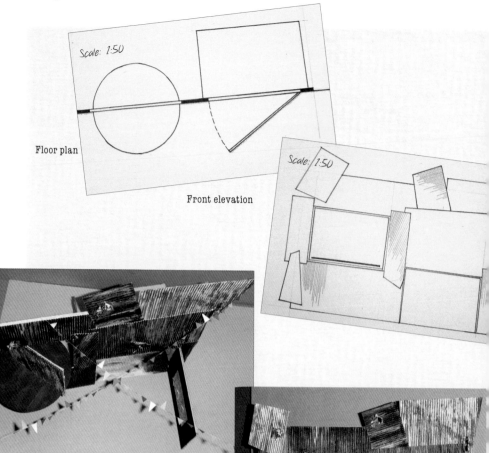

Scale: 1:50

Floor plan

Front elevation

Scale: 1:50

Make a floor plan, elevation, and maquette

Study the first scene from a film of your choice. Now draw a floor plan of the scene, including as much detail as possible (see the floor plan in the panel, right, for an example).

Maquette photographed from above to show how the set articulates, and from the front showing possible textural surface effects.

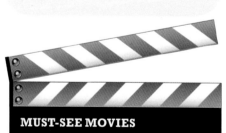

Gothic fantasies
Tim Burton's 2007 movie-musical adaptation of *Sweeney Todd* was an Oscar winner for Art Direction, including set designs by Francesca Lo Schiavo, who superbly conjured a darkly Gothic Victorian England.

Modelmaking

As with storyboards, a maquette and its plans can be as simple or complex as is required by the director. The more detail shown, the easier it is to convey the visual concept to the crew members. Using a maquette, it is possible to work out the spatial relationships, volume, and the walkways through the set, as in the maquette example on the left; from this, a simple plan and elevation can be drawn for the set builders (also shown, left).

Another way of working is to draw thumbnail sketches of ideas (right) then make a series of maquettes. Use a desk lamp to explore ideas about lighting the set. Model figures and furniture can also be included to check sizing and methods of moving around the set. Keep a photographic record mounted in a book for comparison and discussion.

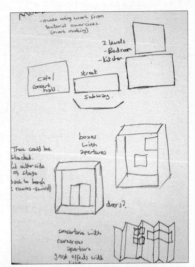

Rough thumbnail sketches prior to maquette

Maquette with figures

Lighting options

Rough thumbnail sketches

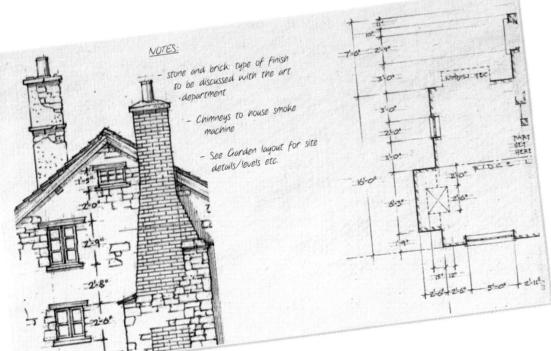

NOTES:
- stone and brick: type of finish to be discussed with the art department
- Chimneys to house smoke machine
- See Garden layout for site details/levels etc.

Attention to detail

If specific locations can't be found, buildings, and even entire neighborhoods, have to be constructed. To convey the illusion, tricks—such as smoke machines in the chimney—have to be employed. These must be detailed on the plans (see the written note on the set builder's plans, left).

Props and set dressing

When you have chosen a location, the next step is to customize it by dressing the set. Set dressers remove or conceal unwanted items and add decor and props to help recreate your fictional world, and make it photogenic.

See also:
Makeup, page 78
Wardrobe, page 82

Using two "L"s to frame a scene
Use two "L" shapes cut from cardboard to frame a scene; manipulate them to make the aperture larger or smaller. Or if you don't have materials handy, simply form two "L"s with your fingers to form a rectangle to make a good makeshift viewfinder to frame a scene.

When dressing a set, inappropriate components can be disguised with drapes, flags, or banners. Suggestive props like a cobbled floor surface or barnyard hay can be added. Unwanted elements that can't be removed, such as automobiles, smokestacks, and company signs, can be carefully masked.

Framing your location

Each location is a collection of potentially stunning and visually appealing backdrops for the movie you are about to create. Directors use a viewfinder to quickly preview proposed frames. Professional models are expensive, but you can make your own for a dime. You can experiment with different sizes. Try making a viewfinder roughly the size of a cell phone that slips easily into your pocket. To use your viewfinder, isolate potential setups in the cut out window. "Zoom" by moving the cardboard nearer to or farther from your eye. Looking at the frames at your location or set carefully, you can then plan how you think the action will take place.

PROJECT 81

Making a director's viewfinder

You will need:
■ letter size sheet of mat board
■ ruler
■ craft knife

1 Draw a 2 in (5 cm) margin on one side and along the top of the board to form a rectangle to the format size you are shooting on (see page 54), such as 4 x 3; 1:185.

2 Draw a 2 in (5 cm) border around the other two sides of your rectangle.

3 Add a handle in the middle of the long side.

4 Cut out carefully.

Props

There are two main categories of props— action props and dressing props.

Action props

Action props are props touched and used by the actors. Items like wallets, dummy credit cards, toothbrushes, hairbrushes, newspapers, and magazines are common props. Items like cigarettes and candles need to have duplicates, as they will likely be reused during the shoot.

Action props are handled by a props master who authorizes use of the props and makes sure they are in the right place ready for the actors to use. The props master will also develop a detailed organization scheme so the props can be tracked and prepared for each day of the shoot, and delivered to the shoot location.

Dressing props

All other props are called dressing props. These could include bespoke furniture or pictures needed to dress a set.

Finding the right prop is a time-consuming chore. Specialty companies will rent unusual props. Other props can be made. When using newspapers and

Staging

PROJECT 82

A single set or location that is tightly framed can become very constricting, claustrophobic, and visually limited. You can use the power of the movie frame to expand beyond your set by following three simple tricks:

- Compose your shots so that set elements bleed out of the frame. Even if they extend only a foot or so in real life, they'll look as though they continue on indefinitely. To enhance the effect, shoot diagonally wherever possible to sell a feeling of depth.

- Block your action so that subjects enter and leave the frame. This reinforces the feeling that their environment continues beyond what viewers can see. When blocking entrances and exits, make sure your screen directions enable the editor to cut different real-world locales together easily.

- Have your actors react to elements that are off screen. If the actors crane their necks to look at someone in the distance, for example, it will give the impression that your set or location extends far beyond what is built and visible.

Set elements to bleed out of frame
This sushi bar may, in fact, be very narrow, but by avoiding each end on film, it looks like it could go on forever.

Actors reacting to elements off screen
Notice how these characters gaze slightly upward, adding depth to the off-screen object of focus.

---

magazines, make sure you have clearances, or get a graphic designer to mock up dummies with a color printer.

Remember that no scene can be shot until all the props are in place. That shot with an actor taking a $100 bill out of his wallet can't happen until the props (the wallet and bill) are in place.

Special needs props
Certain props require extra care. A goldfish bowl with live fish will need daily attention, as will breakaway glass panes and bottles, animals, automobiles, dead bodies, and computer monitors. Water from a faucet requires plumbing, and electric fires and heaters require wiring. Sometimes the location will have wiring and plumbing; other times they will need to be installed.

Crucial props
The plot may revolve around a particular prop. If the prop looks unbelievable, the audience will laugh at the amateurish quality of your film. For example, if the actor brandishes a samurai sword that looks flimsy or plastic, the illusion will be destroyed. Make certain your props look very good—or write them out of the script.

Set dressing

Tonal palette
The production designer may decide on an overall color palette with a number of schemes for use within individual scenes or over the entire movie. Sometimes this can become part of the schedule, as in Ridley Scott's *Alien*. The movie was shot in chronological order with the bright and shiny sets becoming progressively dirty. The set dressing team gradually toned the set down as the movie was shot. Scott carried a can of touch-up paint himself so he could quickly age a detail of the set.

Try to avoid a riot of color that can confuse the eye. Choose colors that will enhance the story. Look at *American Beauty*. Whenever the color red appears, it is never an accident.

Make a list

PROJECT 83

Reread the script, drawing up a list of props that are needed. Then go through the list with a pen and excise all the nonessential items. When you are on a budget, all expenses need to be kept to a minimum and paring down a props list is one way to go about doing this.

Return everything

PROJECT 84

Make a list of everything you have borrowed or rented. List the locations that they have to be returned to, create a schedule. Make a schedule of things you need to fix: painting, filling in holes in walls or ceilings, and so on.

Makeup

Makeup is an important aid to the actor's characterization. The professional tips given here will help you create a variety of looks from basic to unique character effects.

See also:
Wardrobe, page 82

Materials
You'll need a good selection of makeup in a range of colors for different skin tones and ages.

The makeup design sheet (below) for a 1920s-style makeup look (above).

1920S

Hair Water-wave set with cologne off to one side.

Black shadow rounded over lids.

lips blocked out & re-shaped into classic 'bow'

Makeup is deemed necessary because an unmade-up face can look washed out and shiny, detracting from the actor's performance. Makeup in film can enhance the storytelling. It should help actors feel comfortable in character and confident in their acting. Many actors sit down in the makeup chair as themselves and the moment they leave the makeup room go into character until the makeup comes off at the end of the day.

Planning the looks
Makeup for each character and scene should be planned thoroughly.
- Break down the script for each character and scene. This will give you an overview of any effects needed and a feel for each character.
- Ascertain the basic looks required for each character— when and where the action will be set, and the age and style of the character.
- Discuss camera and lighting, as makeup may need to be toned down or intensified to suit.

Makeup and maintenance
If possible, makeup applications should be carried out in a dark room in front of a lit-up mirror. Use a clean set of brushes for each actor to reduce the risk of cross-contamination. Keep shine and red to a minimum, as these can be greatly exaggerated on camera.

Once the makeup is complete, it should be maintained to look as close to the first application as possible throughout the scene. Take photographs for every character's makeup for each scene to ensure accurate makeup continuity.

Creating authentic wounds

Research all makeup thoroughly to ensure authenticity. Use an accurate source to ensure that the period is true to original styling. To do your research, go online, to the library, or a public art gallery. Thorough research is also required for wound makeup.

- Look into the circumstances—how and where the wound occurred and how it will progress—color changes, and so on. You can use design sheets, if you wish, to map the changes.
- Think about where the wound should be placed. More static areas work best. Elbow creases, for instance, can be high maintenance, as friction and skin warmth can cause the makeup to break down.
- Think about hiding the edges of a wound so that it looks more real. Placing a cut through a brow, for example, can draw the eye away from the edges of the wound to the center, making the effects more believable.

Makeup checklist: before the shoot

When you're filming on a budget, you're unlikely to be able to afford to call in a professional. Study the checklist below to ensure you are well prepared.

MAKEUP CHECKLIST
- facial hair removal
- dyeing eyelashes
- brow threading
- tanning
- allergy testing
- Test makeup

It is essential to carry out allergy testing for any product applied to the skin. Immediately remove any makeup if the actor feels any discomfort, burning, or itching.

Female makeup: natural

Beauty makeup, or straight corrective makeup, is about enhancing and balancing a person's face to look her best but without overglamorizing. Skin should be clean and, if possible, primed prior to makeup application. Foundation should create an even-toned, healthy-looking complexion. All visible skin should match and look even. Find a willing volunteer to practice on.

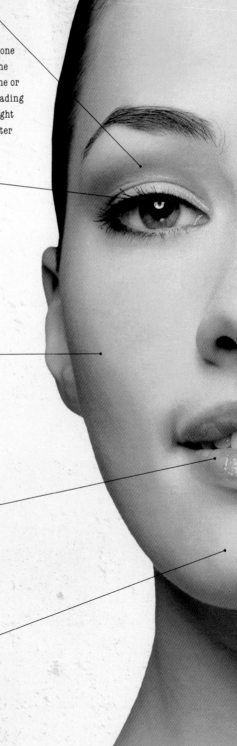

Shading and contouring (step 2)
Sculpt the face and even out features. Shading should be one or two shades darker than the base; highlights should be one or two shades lighter. Apply shading to the receding parts, highlight bone structure with the lighter shade.

Eyes (step 4)
Apply a skin-tone base color over the eye area. Add a highlight to the brow-bone and a mid-tone over the entire lid area. Add tone to the crease above the lid. Apply a brown or black eye liner then mascara.

Cheeks (step 3)
Apply a natural-looking blusher to the apple of the cheeks. To find the apple, either feel for the top of the cheekbones or ask the person to smile.

Lips (step 5)
Balance and define the lip shape with a liner. Fill in the lips with the liner. Apply lipstick evenly with a brush.

The base (step 1)
Apply foundation to the forehead and blend down to cover the entire face. Blend to the ears and down the neck. Apply concealer under the eyes to take away dark circles or hide shadows. Set with powder.

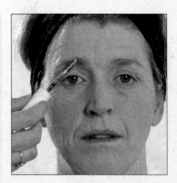

Aging with makeup

If possible, use your subject's family photographs to get an idea of what he or she might look like during the aging process. You can also use an overhead light to see where the natural shadows are cast on the face. Shading under an overhead light creates the illusion of the skin being dragged down, which is a natural progression of the skin during the aging process. This sequence shows an actor being made up using a product called "Old-Age Stipple" (liquid latex).

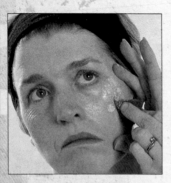
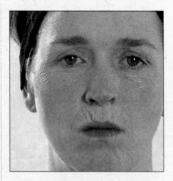
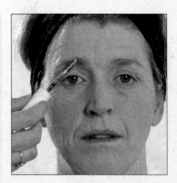

1 Applying Old-Age Stipple
Pour some latex into a saucer ready to use, and tone the face. You must stretch the skin you want to wrinkle before you apply the latex, so do that with one hand and sponge on the latex with the other. Holding the skin, dry it with a dryer set on cool.

2 Creating eye wrinkles
The eye area is particularly important as the skin there loosens early in our lives. Stretch the delicate skin gently, lifting the eyebrows to work on the browbone, being careful not to drip latex into the eyes. You can build up two or three layers of latex, but make sure they don't have thick edges. In tight areas, paint it on with a brush.

3 Creating mouth wrinkles
To help stretch the mouth, pad inside the top and bottom lips with large pieces of sponge, stipple on the latex, and dry. When you take the sponge out, the mouth will look lined.

4 Eyebrows
When you have stippled the mouth, cheeks, forehead, and between brows, color the face. Use shading mixed with a little gray and a few shades darker than the natural skin color. Whiten the eyebrows with a few gray hairs.

Create surface wounds

To create raised effects on the skin, you can buy scar-making material or use eyelash glue. In addition, you'll need mortician's wax or putty, rigid collodion, and gelatin for some of these techniques.

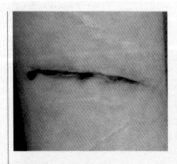

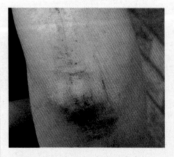

For new scars:
1. Sculpt eyelash glue or scar-making material onto the desired area.
2. Powder this before it has time to dry. You can use a hairdryer to speed up the process. When the glue goes clear, it is dry and ready for makeup.
3. Apply a wash of red around the outside to make the scar look sore.

For old scars:
1. Paint collodion onto the skin and allow to dry. The area will be puckered.
2. Repeat application of collodion to intensify the scar.
3. Discoloration can be applied as for new scars, but scars are usually less red as time goes by.

For scratches:
1. Dip a pin into eyelash glue and run glue over the desired area in different directions.
2. Apply powder.
3. Dip a stipple sponge in red-brown grease and run through the glued area.
4. Paint red washes sporadically.

5 Finishing the face
Apply a little blusher to suggest a rouged face. Use brownish-black mascara. It should not be noticeable.

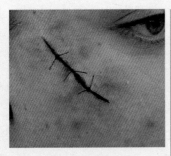

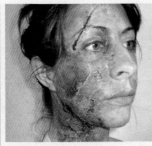

For stitched wounds:
1. Double-tie small black knots of thread.
2. Smooth the wax onto the skin.
3. Create a groove down the center of the wound and roll the edges toward each other to create a pulled-in effect.
4. Press the stitches into the wax, spacing them evenly. Add a red color wash to the wound.

For burns and blisters:
1. Mix gelatin with water and heat as instructed on the packet.
2. Allow to cool slightly.
3. Stipple gelatin onto the skin, and dry with a hairdryer on a low setting.
4. Build up layers of gelatin depending on the severity of the burn.
5. Color areas in with washes of red makeup.

PROJECT 90

Male makeup: natural

Straight corrective male makeup should be kept to a minimum and look natural. Practice the following steps on a willing participant.

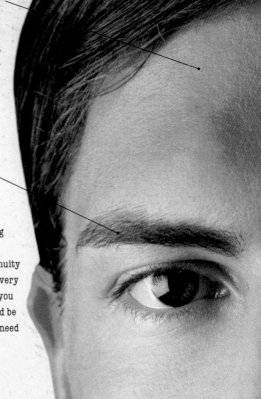
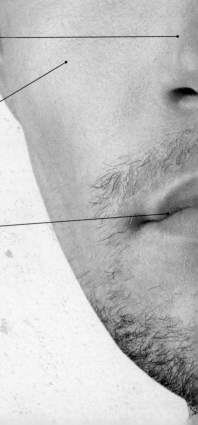

Base (step 1)
Apply foundation, or base, where needed to even out skin tone. Even skin tone on the ears, neck, and any other visible skin.

Eyes and brows (step 2)
Conceal dark shadows, including beard shadows, if required for continuity purposes. Apply a very subtle lash line if you wish. Brows should be groomed and may need to be trimmed.

Shading and contouring (step 3 optional)
Apply shading if you wish.

Cheeks (step 4)
Use a natural blush or bronzer to warm up the complexion.

Lips (step 5)
Apply balm to the lips if you wish. If the lips are very pale, apply a light wash of natural color.

Wardrobe

Creative use of wardrobe allows a filmmaker to add production values to the film. Skillful use of wardrobe is the simplest way to transport an audience to a heightened reality, either in the distant past (or future) or present day. A good wardrobe designer can make pleasing and exciting wardrobes using basic materials without breaking the budget.

See also:
Makeup, page 78

All dressed up

Although every production is different, the basic rules and requirements remain the same. If your shoot is going to last more than one day, you will need a person to run your wardrobe. Even if your actors are supplying their own costumes, you need someone to coordinate the logistics. When a shoot lasts longer than a day, it is especially important that actors do not wear their costumes to the shoot—they must be left with the wardrobe person. Allowing actors to leave the shoot in their costumes is courting disaster, as the clothes risk being dirtied or, worse, being left at home. Polaroids were a standard tool of costume departments, used to keep a record of who wore what and how, but digital still cameras are more convenient, economical, and efficient, especially if used with a laptop computer.

Apart from the organizational aspect, the wardrobe person/ department has to work in conjunction with the production designer. Not only do the costumes have to fit the characters, but the choice of colors and patterns can influence the look and meaning of the finished movie. For example, in Warren Beatty's *Dick Tracy*, the costumes used bold, flat colors to enhance the overall "comic book" look of the film. They are subtle details that may go unnoticed but do make a difference, just as giving a character a particular color to wear can add symbolic meaning.

Getting the wardrobe and makeup organized before the shoot, even if it's a guerrilla-style movie, will make everything run that much more smoothly on the day of filming.

Area of responsibility
On big budget films, the costume department is responsible for clothing, accessories, footwear, underwear, hats, and wigs.

PROJECT 91

Figure out what you need

Decide what the types of costumes are in your film. What can be supplied by the actors, and what will need to be made or rented.

For example, if your script calls for a jogging suit, chances are your actor will have one. But if the jogging suit is a uniform, like the football or cheerleading team, then it will have to be made, borrowed, or rented.

Action
Actors in costume at colonial Williamsburg, Virginia (above).

PROJECT 92

Interpret some reference

Suppose the director showed you this picture (left) as a reference photograph. How would you make a costume for an actress matching this? Where would you find an apron? Could you make one? How much would the fabric cost? Make notes for how you would create this costume. A good place to start would be by sketching your ideas for the costume, then gathering fabric swatches to use in the costume (left below).

eyelet fastenings

large pockets on sides

PROJECT 93

Thrift store finds

Period costumes can be expensive. Pick one of the following periods and see if you can make a costume for one actor using thrift store finds that look convincing but won't break the budget.

- 1990s Yuppie
- 1960s Flower Child
- 1770s War of Independence

MUST-SEE MOVIES

★ *THE DUCHESS* (2008)
Key Players: Director: Saul Dibb; Costume Designer: Michael O'Connor.
Won the Oscar for Best Costume Design in 2008.

★ *THE CURIOUS CASE OF BENJAMIN BUTTON* (2008)
Key Players: Director: David Fincher; Costume Designer: Jacqueline West.
Costumes over the lifespan of a man aging backward.

Low-budget special effects

You may not have A-list stars or be shooting on 35 mm film, you've probably not got any helicopter shots lined up, and it's doubtful you can afford a monster, but there's one place your production value can shine, and, if you're making horror, one place it must do so.

Of course, there will always be the less-is-more school of thought, but if your project is more *Bad Taste* than *Cat People*, you'll be wanting to make fake limbs and lots of blood. Page 86 covers some basic blood tricks and provides you with the methods used to make a variety of fake body parts. The example chosen is a severed hand, but the methods described are transferable and the difficulty is in the extras. Once you know about the materials it's all quite easy.

Who's who in special effects

Stunt Coordinator
Makes sure that any stunt involving people is safe and photogenic (falling off a roof, tripping down stairs, brawls, fist fights, and so on).

Special Effects Coordinator
Makes sure that any special effect is carried out correctly and safely (gunshots, car crashes, any inanimate object that has to move on its own).

A few words on blood
Fake blood is expensive, but it's often worth it. The recipes you find for home brews are often not as good as the better store-bought stuff. However, the recipe given on page 86 is actually rather good. It's better used in volume, where you'll have pools, as it's not as suited to smears, particularly not on fabric. Also, if you try and keep it for more than a few days, it tends to turn bright green. But at around a fortieth of the price of the better store stuff, it's an invaluable and easy option.

Paper people
Fake bodies, normally made of polyurethane from a fiberglass-reinforced plastic (GRP) mold, with a metal skeleton, run to several thousand dollars each, even for generic models. Here (project 94) is how to make one for under $40.

There are limitless uses for this one. Want to see someone fall off a building? Need someone to be hit by a car? This is your prop. Not only that, but it's modular and so can be used to make a great separate arm or leg piece too.

Let it rain
You can make a simple rain machine by drilling holes in a garden hose and suspending it, coiled, on a wooden frame.

PROJECT 94

Make a cheap body
You will need plastic wrap, masking tape, gaffer tape, a willing victim/model, and several newspapers, as well as marker pen, scissors, and a steady hand.

Body parts
You need to think about the body as being made up of several moveable parts—fifteen of them to be precise. Here is the list:
1. head
2. upper torso
3. lower torso/pelvis
4. left upper arm
5. right upper arm
6. left forearm
7. right forearm
8. left hand
9. right hand
10. left thigh
11. right thigh
12. left lower leg
13. right lower leg
14. left foot
15. right foot

You make each part separately and then put them together to make the fake body.

Select your body part—let's say a lower arm for the sake of this chapter (and because we'll want one later)—and work out where the joints lie. For the lower arm they are the elbow and the wrist; elsewhere they should be suitably obvious. Wrap the model's body part in plastic wrap (you can go well past the edges) and then put a strip of gaffer tape over the wrap along the outside edge of the body. Use a longer piece than you need—it'll make your life easier. You'll need to be able to get scissors in there later, so chose an area that's as accessible as possible. On the lower arm go from elbow to little finger.

Now rewrap the part in plastic wrap. Once done, it's time for the masking tape. You can use gaffer for this step too, but in the interests of cost, settle for a good quality paper tape. It needs to stick to itself, so the cheap stuff is a no-go.

Is it a man? Is it a fake?

A clip from *Hooper* (1978). The flying figure looks like a Burt Reynolds stunt double but why bother with flesh and blood stunt people, when you can make your own fake figure and subject it to every kind of indignity?

Cover the selected part in tape. It's best to use lengthwise strips and then reinforce with pieces wrapped around, but be careful not to go too tight with these as a) you need to be able to get this off later and b) you want to avoid gangrene in your model.

Note that the process of joining this cost-cutter Frankenstein's monster together tends to lengthen the limbs somewhat, so you can afford to lose a little off each section to take this into account.

When the tape is on, mark the surface with a line, showing where the gaffer is. Then, intersect this with little crosses every inch or so—this will help you put the piece back together. Carefully cut the tape with the scissors, following your line and using the gaffer to protect the skin.

Once off, trim the edges to remove any jagged bits and carefully tape back together. Close off one end of what will now be a tube with more tape, being careful not to disfigure or squash the forearm. Now stuff it tightly with balls of newspaper until full. Cap off with yet more tape and put aside, clearly marked, before starting on the next piece. Once you have all your pieces made, you can assemble them, using gaffer to create hinge joints for the knees and elbows, and gaffer and string to make more universal joints for everything else.

With the head, it may be worth using a polystyrene wig head, as they're cheap and it saves the hassle of making a tape one (easily the trickiest part). If you do decide to make a tape head, leave the mouth open while the model's wrapped in plastic wrap. Also, bend their head forward a little while making it so the back of the neck is more conducive to cutting the tape when you come to remove it.

Now that it's put together, dress it in costume and throw it off a cliff. On camera.

Added extras

If you want to make the body a little more rugged, you can run a dowel through each of the body parts, screwing rope in or adding hinges where appropriate. Also, a cheap mask from a Halloween or party store can make all the difference to the guy as he sails down the side of that tower block.

If you want a close-up of a limb breaking, it's good to put a length of balsa in the joint to provide resistance. This is also useful if you need to make a dummy stand up; balsa is strong enough to make him rigid but will snap when he's hit at 40 mph by your brother's Volvo. You'll need a stand though; these things have terrible balance.

Body search

Check out some movies for examples of fake bodies.

■ **Where you can see them low budget:**
Peter Jackson's *Bad Taste,* when Derek
falls off the cliff.

■ **Where you can see them high budget:**
The high-budget ones are much more expensive but should give
you some ideas. One of the best dummy heavy movies is the
Steven Seagal vehicle *Exit Wounds*, which features several cop
dummies being run over or crushed.

Make your own blood

Store-bought fake blood is expensive. Try making
your own using the recipe, below.

Realistic blood recipe

Ingredients

arrowroot (secret ingredient number 1)
red, black, green, yellow, and blue food coloring
coffee (secret ingredient number 2)

Incidentally, an added advantage of this recipe is that it
contains no sugar, so when you're shooting horror outside
in the summer, your shrieking starlet is less likely to
get covered in wasps and ants. The trick with arrowroot
is to have patience.

1. Measure out your water
and put it in a pan over a low
heat. Separately mix up your
arrowroot with a little bit of
water to make a concentrate.
You want about 2 teaspoons of
arrowroot per 8 fl. oz (250ml)
of blood (water at this point).
Pour this into the still cool
water in the pan. Slowly heat
up your mix and—this next bit
is important—stir constantly.
Any hot spots forming in your
pan will cause clots (actually
a neat and useful defect if you
precolor your water).

2. Unless you want clots, add
the color when the mixture is
warm, before it gets too thick.
Start with the red; obviously
this'll be your main color.
The regular stuff you find in
supermarkets in this country
can be too pinky if you don't
use enough. Food coloring
paste, found in baking supply
stores, may be a better option.

3. Next is the blue—not too
much, just to darken. A tiny,
tiny bit of yellow and green
will help add that brown edge

that blood has. The black can
bring it down further but
check the color base of the
black—all black food coloring
is just very dark something
else. Greeny blacks are better
than bluey blacks for blood. It's
worth noting that venal blood
is darker than arterial blood,
so if you want realism, fatal
wounds, normally sustained
to arteries like the carotid
or the femoral, tend to bleed
a brighter, more Herschell
Gordon Lewis color.

4. The coffee is another
thing used to bring down the
brightness because, for all
my warbling about the colors
of blood from different body
parts, the favorite these days
is glassy, dark blood, almost
black. You've got to admit; it
looks great in pools.

5. Bring the entire mixture
to a near boil, having been
stirring constantly, and then
take it off the heat. As it cools
it will thicken up, giving you
a nice viscous blood, great
for pools and set dressing.

Use within two days as
some coloring goes funny in
arrowroot and you may come
back to a batch and find it has
turned bright green. If it's too
thick, just water it down, but
too much water and you'll need
to up the color. Remember, this
stuff will stain skin and may
not wash out of clothing.

6. Now fill some condoms
with the stuff and put them in
the dummy before his rooftop
dive. (Little bits of sponge with
thumbtacks in them taped to
condoms or balloons will cause
them to pop when under
pressure or impact.)

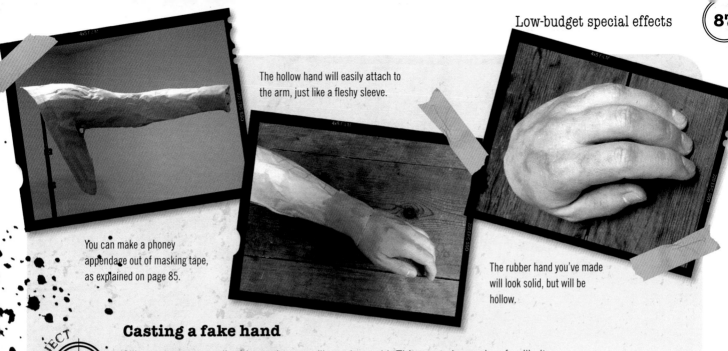

The hollow hand will easily attach to the arm, just like a fleshy sleeve.

You can make a phoney appendage out of masking tape, as explained on page 85.

The rubber hand you've made will look solid, but will be hollow.

Casting a fake hand

PROJECT 97

Silicone comes as a liquid or gel, so you'll need a mold. This example requires familiarity with another new material, alginate. Alginate is the stuff they use to make casts of your teeth at the dentist and is totally skin-safe and nontoxic. It is a powder and needs to be mixed with water—each brand comes with instructions regarding the ratio.

1 Experiment with small volumes before you make the hand because it's fast-setting stuff.
   If your model has hairy wrists, slather them in a water-based moisturizer before you start. Make a cardboard tube and fill it with alginate mix (a thick paste). Get the model to push his hand into the tube and wiggle it around to ensure coverage.

2 Have your model take the position you want your fake hand to have, ensuring the hand is not touching the edges of the tube. After a few minutes the alginate will have set and the model can pull the hand out. This should be achievable without cutting the alginate. Once air starts to get into the mold, the hand will slide out with a lovely sucking noise.

3 Now that you have your mold you'll want to fill it with rubber. There are several different materials available. You need to ensure you use a translucent rubber (for aesthetics; the other option is white) and a tin or condensation cure rubber (for cost the other option is platinum or addition cure). Recommended is TinGel 10 (from Polytek in the US and from Mouldlife in the UK). The rubber has two parts, the monomer (the thick part) and the catalyst (the thin part). These will need to be mixed to a ratio specified by the manufacturer. However, silicone can be rather slow to set, so you can either over-catalyze or use an accelerator, available as a separate chemical from the supplier. TinGel 10 has a 16-hour cure (set) time, but can be made to be ready in about 15 minutes with the accelerator. Bear in mind that the longer you allow the rubber to cure, the longer any bubbles will have to rise to the top, i.e., the wrist end.

4 You'll want to color the rubber too, before you pour it (this is called intrinsic coloration). You can buy pigments to make your own skin color, and premixed skin tone is also available. Err on the side of less pigment, as the advantage of silicone is its translucency and you don't want to spoil that with too much pigment.

5 Now you can tear apart the alginate to get at the hand and, trust me, it'll be awesome.

Silicone search

PROJECT 98

Check out some movies to see silicone parts in action.

■ Where you can see them low budget:
The *Guinea Pig* films were the first to use silicone; it was so real that some people believed that the second one was a snuff movie.

■ Where you can see them high budget:
In *JFK*, the nude corpse is entirely silicone—made by the excellent Gordon Smith.

Lights, cell phone, action

Cell phones are an exciting and accessible way to record and show your work. However, to shoot a movie that is suited to such a small screen, you need to understand a few basic principles.

See also
Choosing and using the camera, page 41
Sound, page 48

You can use any cell phone that can record movies to shoot your film. The advantages are clear: You can shoot in locations and in situations where a larger camera might not be feasible and the camera is free if you have the right service contract with your favorite telephone network. The disadvantages are the lack of picture quality (although this is improving all the time) and having to record sound onto a separate device. The tips below will help you produce a more professional-looking movie.

Media-savvy cell
Cell phones, such as the Nokia N Series, were designed to be media-savvy, for both capturing and playing back video.

RULES FOR CELL PHONE SHOOTING

1 No wide shots
Shots where the main subject is 50 yards away won't "read" as well as shots closer up. Try to keep as close to the subject as possible.

2 No fast movements
Any quick or sudden movement will cause the image to pixelate, and thus be very difficult for your viewer to watch.

3 Avoid low light levels
Cell phones work best in bright light. Low light levels can cause grainy images. Point lamps or open curtains before you start shooting to get the most light possible and thus the best image.

4 Light source
Keep the brightest light source behind the videographer. Don't put a subject in front of a bright window, unless you want a blackened silhouette.

5 Don't depend on sound to tell your story
Recording audio on your cell phone can

be a problem. Titles are a good way to convey your storyline. Keep them simple—one to three words are best.

6 Avoid whip pans
Whip pans might look great in a Tarantino movie but will make a small-screen viewer seasick. Try to smooth out the shots and get rid of jerky movements.

7 Sound recording
The sound recorded on a camera's microphone may be too low resolution.

Make sure you have the best microphone and sound recording unit possible.

8 Keep the lens clean
Carry a soft cloth and keep your lens free of lint, fingerprints, and grime from the bottom of your pocket.

9 Exit camera left, enter camera right
Because of the way images are loaded onto a cell phone or a website, an actor exiting from the left will look smoother than one exiting from the right. Exit from the right and your actor's image will strobe and jerk as the movement fights against the natural loading of the page. So, too, with actors entering shots. They should always enter camera right, exit camera left. The tests you will carry out in project 99 (right) should give you a chance to see this for yourself.

Camera vs. cell tests

Use your camera to do the following tests, then repeat the tests using your cell phone.

- Have a friend walk toward your camera from 20 yards away. Keep him in focus.

- Have a friend run into the frame from the right, then run in from the left. In line with rule 9 (left), the latter looks much less smooth than the former.

- Have a friend stand directly in front of your camera. Execute a whip pan from the left or right (90 degrees).

- Repeat with the light source in your eyes, and to your back.

Test shots
These pictures were taken with a camera. Compare the results with ones taken on your cell phone.

20 yards

Enter left

10 yards

Center

2 yards

Exit right

View your camera tests

Upload your camera tests and your cell phone tests to *Youtube.com*, *dailymotion.com*, or another video-sharing site, and watch your tests played back. Note and comment under the following categories:

- Sound
- Picture clarity
- Smoothness
- Ease of upload

How did they differ?

Cell phone music video
The Presidents of the United States of America filmed their music video for *Some Postman* entirely using a rig of Sony Ericsson cell phones.

Editing & Post-production

The editor's job is to take the images and sounds collected in the shoot and combine them in a way that he or she feels best tells the story represented by the script. The editor makes notes on each film rush, and from that creates an **Edit Decision List**. It is from this **EDL** that a technician will know which footage from the shoot needs to be saved, which pieces can be discarded, and in which order the rushes run.

An editor is highly skilled in assimilating all of the rushes. A good editor has a strong visual eye and the ability to combine moving pictures with sound effects and music—this process is known as post-production.

Editing

The editor is one of the four key creatives on a film, along with the writer, actors, and director. The editor's input can greatly enhance a movie. Make sure you meet your editor as soon as possible, preferably at script stage. He or she will have invaluable advice on how and what to shoot in order to tell your story effectively.

See also
Storyboarding, page 28
How to shoot a movie, page 58

The Edit Decision List

It is the editor's job to create the Edit Decision List (EDL). To create the EDL, the editor previews all the rushes and looks at the camera reports. Once the editor has a good idea of what the rushes are, she makes a paper edit by noting in writing what the best shots are. At some point, the editor rereads the script. She discusses ideas about the script and the rushes with the director and then begins editing. This stage is called the rough assembly. After further discussions with the director, the editor fine-tunes the film. This stage is called the fine cut. After more discussions and possible amendments, the picture is "locked," meaning there will be no further changes to the images. The time code corresponding to each cut is then exported and is called the EDL.

Using B Roll

B roll is the term used for alternative footage shot during the shoot, often without sound. It is an effective way to hide unwanted zooms or blips shot from the main camera.

In documentaries, if a speaker has any nervous ticks, the ticks can be removed by cutting to B roll footage of what the person is talking about. Sometimes producers or directors of documentaries use B roll to edit statements and take them out of context. In drama, B roll, sometimes called cutaways, can be used to indicate simultaneous action or flashbacks, usually to increase tension or reveal story or character information to the viewer.

Main footage

PROJECT 101

B roll

Edited roll

Every picture tells a story

When shooting, it is useful to capture additional footage—either from a second camera or by placing the single camera in a second position, taking a wider shot of the scene. This second camera produces B roll, allowing the editor additional choices, as in the edited roll, below.

Editing on your computer

If you have a PC with Windows XP, it's almost certain that you'll have Windows Movie Maker preinstalled; on Apple computers the freebie is iMovie. Both programs are designed to make editing easy and straightforward. Most editing programs have trials and free tutorials available online, offering training that was totally unavailable a few years ago. Use them.

Types of cuts

There are many kinds of cuts, but the main ones are a straight cut between scenes, dissolves, fade-outs, and fade-ins. Your editing software will have most of these cutting features (sometimes called transitions) preinstalled.

Paper edit

Review your rushes and make a note of the time code of the best shots. Write these down on paper, along with your ideas about the sequence they should play in.

Be organized!

If you've used a storyboard to make your film, give each scene that you've shot and downloaded to your computer the same name it had on the storyboard. This will make putting the film together during editing much easier.

Continuity

If your main character has yellow socks in the beginning of a scene, be sure that they don't change to black halfway through.

In-camera editing

The editing stage can be bypassed through clever use of the camera. By stopping and starting at the right times, a movie can, in theory, be made without editing at all, as demonstrated by the hilarious annual Straight-8 film competition.

Cuts and transitions

For this project you will need a computer with a basic editing software package, and several short pieces of film imported into your computer. Splices in a film are called cuts because in traditional filmmaking the filmstrips were cut manually with a razor blade and taped together. More complicated cuts involving fades and dissolves were done in a film lab. Some computer programs call these transitions. Make the following cuts using your footage:

■ **Jump cut:** A series of very quick and jerky cuts in which several seconds of a scene of action are thrown away.

■ **Dissolve:** A transition between two shots, where one shot fades away and another shot fades in (below).

■ **Fade:** A transition from a shot to black where the image gradually becomes darker is a fade-out; or from black where the image gradually becomes brighter is a fade-in (shown, below).

■ **Match cut:** A cut on a specific point of action, for example a handshake, where it is shot from one side and then again from another side. The actors try and make the same movement, so it can be matched in the edit, as in match cut.

Cutting your losses

In-camera editing is useful if you have limited film stock, but it doesn't leave much room for error or alternatives when doing the final cut, and it needs careful planning. Shooting lots of coverage gives you more editing choices to explore the scene, but it can introduce continuity.

Example 1

1A WIDE SHOT: The camera captures a man in a field.

1B MEDIUM SHOT: The camera pans in and around to show the man closer and reveal the approaching car.

Example 2

2A WIDE SHOT: Camera cuts to diner and shoots both friends eating.

2B CLOSE-UP The camera zooms in to show just one friend.

PROJECT 103

In-camera editing

Shoot a scene involving several different shots in-camera (see above). Any of the following would make good scenes to shoot: someone getting ready to go out, cooking, grooming a family pet, eating a meal. Play the scene back to see if the cuts make sense. If they don't, redo them until the transitions are smooth.

PROJECT 104

Parallel cutting

Prepare two short shots: one of someone staring into the distance, and the second of a landscape or cityscape. Take the shots on different days and in different locations. Cut the two together to make it look as though they were shot in the same area on the same day.

PROJECT 105

Spot the mistake

Watching for continuity errors has become a sport for hundreds of thousands of movie fanatics. *Premiere* magazine carries a monthly feature called "Gaffe Squad," in which readers point out continuity errors in popular commercial movies. An Internet search for film continuity errors yields hundreds of websites dedicated to picking movies apart. The Internet Movie Database Goofs page (*www.imdb.com/Sections/Goofs*) is probably the largest collection of viewer-submitted movie errors ever assembled. Now see if you can spot the continuity glitches in the following scenes:

1. **Raiders of the Lost Ark**—the firefight in Marion's bar.
2. **Back to the Future**—George and Marty talking at the clothesline.
3. **Pulp Fiction**—the army guy giving Butch the watch.
4. **Jurassic Park**—the helicopter landing on the island.
5. **Titanic**—Captain Smith ordering Murdoch to take the ship to sea.
6. **The Shining**—Jack Nicholson chopping out a door panel.

Answers:

1. Indy's gun changes from a .38 revolver to a Colt .45, back to a .38, then back once again to a .45. This explains why he is able to fire his gun seven times with every loading.
2. Both of Marty's shirt pocket flaps are out, but in the next shot one of them is tucked in.
3. The time changes twice as the watch is flipped over in Butch's hand.
4. As the helicopter lands, we get an overhead view of the landing area, featuring a waterfall and two jeeps waiting to take the passengers to the visitors' center. But when we see the ground-level view of the helicopter landing in the next shot, we see the jeeps backing up to the position they were already in just before.
5. When Captain Smith orders, "Take her to sea, Mr. Murdoch—let's stretch her legs," they are standing to the right of the wheelhouse looking forward with the sun coming from their left. As Murdoch walks into the wheelhouse to carry out the order, the sun is behind him.
6. We see Jack Nicholson chop apart only one of the door panels with his ax—and yet after we see him listen to the arrival of the snowcat, both panels are chopped.

Example 3

Example 4

3A WIDE SHOT: The camera shows the couple laying in bed.

3B CLOSE-UP: The camera zooms in to show just their faces.

4A WIDE SHOT: Scene cuts to show the man sitting on the sidewalk.

4B MEDUIM SHOT: Camera then zooms to focus more on his face and upper body.

Harrison Ford, as the iconic Indiana Jones, gets all fired up for another fight in *Raiders of the Lost Ark*.

Sound and music

Most of the sound and music heard on the screen in theaters has been recreated in post-production sound editing.

See also:
Sound, page 48

Another tool filmmakers use to create images is sound. The way our minds combine images and sounds makes cinema the most exciting of the arts.

Traditional filmmaking involves recording the sounds and dialogue during the shoot. This material serves as a guide and backup, and is thrown away as the sounds are recreated in a process known as sweetening the sound track. There are many lessons to be learned from this for first-time filmmakers.

Automated Dialogue Replacement

Automated Dialogue Replacement or Additional Dialogue Recording (ADR) is a film sound technique involving the rerecording of dialogue after photography. It is also known as looping, a looping session, post-synchronization, or post-sync.

An actor watches the performance on a video playback, and rerecords lines into a high-quality microphone in time to the images. This track is then inserted into the edit.

Creating Foley

Foley artists are named after Jack Foley, one of the earliest and best-known Hollywood practitioners of the art of recreating everyday sound effects to be added to the sound edit. Footsteps, breaking glass, paper rustling, door slams, and body noise are recreated by Foley artists, and recorded in a controlled setting.

Room noise or buzz track

Each room has its own distinct sound. When you have finished shooting a scene, turn the camera off, ask all the actors to stand quietly, leave all lights, fans, and other ambient noise on, and record the sound. This is done to create a matching background for any new material that is inserted into the track, or to fill holes created in the track by the removal of other background noises.

PROJECT **107**

Record rainfall

1 Set up your microphone.
2 Get a package of rice. Pour the rice onto a hard surface like a desk or a piece of sheet metal.
3 Record and play back. It will sound like rainfall.

PROJECT **106**

Make a noise

Even the simplest sound effects can work wonders in transforming a film from the humdrum into an effective and exciting production. A film of a speeding car, for instance, is considerably enhanced by the sound of squealing tires on the soundtrack; if the final shot is a car smash, it will appear far more realistic if the sound of the crash is heard by the audience before they see the wreck of the car. Sound effects can be downloaded from the Internet, or you can create your own effects at home.

Thunder roll
Simulate a roll of thunder by blowing gently on the microphone.

Row boat
Conjure a row boat by coordinating the noise made by a creaky door and the splashing sound made by rhythmically dipping a piece of wood into a bucket full of water.

Listen up

Listen to the sounds in the first minutes of any film, and make a note of what you hear. The description (below) is of the first couple of minutes of Tim Burton's 2001 film *Planet of the Apes* (still, right).

1. Rumble of spaceship
2. Beeping/clicking of spaceship controls
3. Sound of chimp
4. Different beeping
5. Crash sound, as if something banged into spacecraft
6. Chimp bouncing in seat
7. Clicking of control panel switches
8. Different beep
9. Helmet visor opening/closing
10. Beeping
11. Sound of many people talking on radio muffled with interference
12. Sound of large space station/rumble
13. Chimp making noise
14. Footsteps of chimp and human down long hall
15. Many apes making noise, stomping (chimps and orangutans)
16. Xylophone (as if chimp is playing it)

Large bird in flight
Create the effect of a large bird in flight by flapping two pieces of bamboo in front of a microphone.

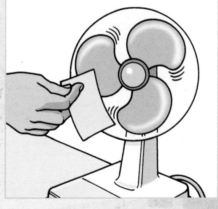

Small fluttering bird
Reproduce the sound of a small bird's wings by recording the sound made when a piece of card stock flutters against a fan.

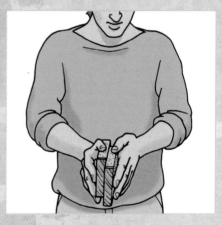

Steam train
If you need the sound of a puffing steam train—say, for a comedy sequence—cover two wooden blocks with sandpaper and rub them together.

Try mixing sounds

Collect all different sound elements (foley, ADR, sound effects, music) and place them into separate audio channels in your editing software (Apple Final Cut, Adobe Premiere). Synchronize them with the picture. Once synchronized, export to an audio program, such as Apple Soundtrack or Adobe Soundbooth—depending upon your editing software, and balance and equalize the sound levels. This is to ensure that one sound doesn't dominate another where inappropriate and the sounds aren't distorted. Good-quality headphones or monitor speakers should be used for this. Getting this right is important because bad sound is more distracting than bad pictures. A screengrab from Final Cut is shown below with key software features identified, including those used for audio transitions.

Browser
Clip references are placed here for easy access. Also, this area has an "effects" tab, which offers video and audio transitions and filters.

Viewer
This is where the selected clip's video and audio parameters can be adjusted according to length, volume, scale, and so on.

Insert
When using an insert edit, the new clip will be inserted into an existing clip in the Timeline. This will preserve the entirety of the existing clip, and move segments of it to the left and right to make room for the new clip.

Canvas
This outputs the contents of the Timeline, allowing you to watch the edited clips. Clips can be added to the Timeline by dragging them to the canvas, which then offers several edits, such as "insert" or "replace."

In and out points
In and out points allow you to define a specific portion of a clip or sequence for editing, deletion, copying, pasting, and so on.

Timeline
This is where the clips are edited together into sequences.

Add marker
Markers are visible points on clips and sequences that can be used for commenting, synchronizing, editing, adding DVD chapter and compression markers, and even making subclips. By default, markers exist only on the frame where they were created, but you can also create markers that have a duration.

Replace
This allows for the replacement of a clip in the timeline without the use of ins or outs. Final Cut will take the placement of the two playheads and automatically time the ins and outs of the replacement movie to the clip that it will replace.

Overwrite
Overwrite edits allow for a new clip to overwrite or replace portions of your existing clip or clips. The portions replaced will be equal to the duration of the new clip you're moving to the Timeline.

Razor blade
The most basic edit is a straight cut, like the ones performed with a razor blade on a piece of film. Each time you cut a clip in your sequence, it is split into two. You can make cuts with the Razor Blade tool on the Timeline, or you can make cuts during playback.

Actors rerecord their dialogue in a soundproof room watching the scene on video screen. The sound engineer uses digital tools to match the sound to the shooting environment.

Music

It is an urban myth that you can have your actor run through a room with up to eight seconds of a Beatles' song playing on the radio for free. Music rights are very expensive, and it can cost more than $100,000 to use a snippet of a Beatles' song. If you do not have permission to use someone else's music in your movie, you won't be able to sell it. Musical scores do not necessarily have to contain songs. The soundtrack to *The Blair Witch Project* used the heartbeats of the actors. Think about creating ambience. You can never use anyone else's music without clearing the rights for it. Even if your best friend composes a soundtrack or musical score for your movie, he or she will need to assign 100 percent of the rights to you or you won't be able to sell your movie anywhere.

Music rights

You need to clear three types of rights —those belonging to the lyricist, the composer, and the performer. Sometimes, as in the case of a singer/songwriter, it is just one person (or the record company). If you use cover versions, or performers producing recordings of other people's lyrics and melodies, it can get more difficult.

To clear an existing recording, contact the record company on the label of the CD. The music company will negotiate a price for the use of the recording that it owns. Original recordings of songs are always more expensive than getting a local musician to rerecord the song as a cover.

To rerecord, you will need to get a synch license from the music publisher, and factor in the cost of booking a professional recording studio and the musicians' time. If you don't know a song's publisher there are several places you can look:

BMI (*www.bmi.com*)
ASCAP (*www.ascap.com*)
ESAC (*www.sesac.com*)

You can search by the following criteria:
- Song title
- Writer
- Publisher
- Artist

Usage

Choosing music requires you to consider the following: Your budget, whether the songs are popular or currently unknown, whether your film is commercial or educational, and where the song is used—on the opening or closing credits, or in a regular scene.

Music rights holders will want to know the answers to the following questions before they offer you a price for the song you wish to use:
- Length. Forty seconds? Two minutes? The whole song?
- Duration of time you want to use the music. A day? A month? A year? This is called the term.
- Territory you want to cover.

PROJECT **110**

Identify the sounds of a room

Listen to the sounds in the room you are in. List them (see the example, below). Can you hear traffic? Phones ringing next door? Is there a heating or air conditioning fan? Does the lightbulb make a hiss? Each sound is unique to your room. It will be the same on the locations and sets you will be using.

BEDROOM SOUNDS

1. Sound of blue jay outside window
2. Truck with snowplow driving toward house and then away
3. Train in the distance
4. Heat clicking on and blowing through heating vent
5. Dog barking
6. Children playing next door

Finishing up

After the hectic shoot and the intense editing and post-production sound period, you are nearly finished. These last few details, if done well, will make all the difference to your success.

See also
The film crew, page 8

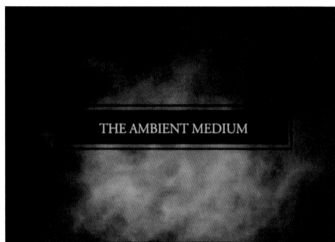

To complete your film so that it is ready for delivery, you need to finish it up.

Titles

There are two types of titles: Opening title credits, which appear at the start, and the rear title crawl, which are the credits at the end of a film. You must include a copyright notice and the year of completion at the end of your film. If it is a fictional work, you might want to include a disclaimer.

Titles are made for films in three ways—in-camera, the Saul Bass method, and the graphic design method.

With the help of the art department you can create a title that is integrated into the setting and becomes part of the story. For example, Bob Dylan's *Don't Look Back* is, in fact, in-camera credits. Other examples are *Napoleon Dynamite* and *High Fidelity*.

Saul Bass became famous for elaborate animated opening title sequences for films such as *North by Northwest* (1959), *Psycho* (1960), and *West Side Story* (1961).

With programs like InDesign, QuarkXPress, or Illustrator, you can compose your own opening title cards, which you can then import into your editing software. When you import the title cards you will need to tell your editor how long

you want each card to appear. You will also have to decide the order of the cards. The director's title card is usually last. Examples of graphic design titles include *When Harry Met Sally*, *As Good as It Gets*, and *Thelma and Louise*.

Opening and closing

The opening title sequence is usually just the creative credits: writers, director, producer, actors. The closing credits show at the end of a film, and list all members of the cast and crew, including those listed in the opening credits. Most often, the closing credits will run vertically on the screen coming up from the bottom.

Who goes where?

There is no convention for credits. The best two opening title credits are first position and last position, and these are decided by negotiation with the talent involved.

Credit style

In the famous title sequence for *Psycho*, Saul Bass uses a series of rapid, gray bars to transition between credits of simple, white text. The title sequence for *Exodus* also employs white text but appears in front of a dark blue background and just

Different approaches
Two different approaches to titling that set the tones of the films. *Cricker Crack* uses hand-drawn notes to impart the casual mood of the movie, while *The Ambient Medium* uses classical typography to give a formal air.

above an illustrated, flickering flame. With illustrations of a black telephone against a red background, the title sequence of *The Human Factor* shows Bass' penchant for simple text imposed over bold backgrounds.

Prints
Trial print
Once the titles, sound effects, and additional special effects have been imported into the Timeline, the end result is viewed at a screening attended by the producer, director, cinematographer, and editor. The post-production process is a huge collation exercise with hundreds, and even thousands of pieces of information needing to be cued up at the right time. Mistakes can happen. This is what the trial print is for. After the screening, necessary changes are made.

Answer print
This is the master copy that all the

Bembo

Mister Frisky

Wilhelm klingspor gotisch

Helvetica neue

The right type

Choosing an appropriate typeface for your opening and closing credits will help to convey the mood of the film. Some examples are shown above.

duplicates will be made from. It is a very precious piece of material and should be stored in a safe place. It is advisable to make several copies of the film at this stage, and keep them in different locations as a backup.

From the answer print, you will make copies for cast and crew, potential distributors, journalists, and film festivals.

Organization

Each film should have its own large file in which you can keep track of all the contracts, licenses, and financial records. If you have set up your own company to make films, you will need to comply with local tax and accounting laws. Running a film production company, even your own, is no different from running any other business in this regard.

PROJECT 111

Useful websites

Most editing software comes with title/credit creation functions. To create something unique, you'll need to use dedicated software such as Adobe After Effects or Apple's Final Cut editing program. There are some great websites on the Internet that allow you to access a vast resource of typographical styles and fonts, and some of them are even free. Check out these software and free font websites.

www.adobe.com/products/aftereffects/main.html
AfterEffects

www.apple.com
LiveType and Motion

www.macromedia.com
Flash

Free typefaces
www.acidfonts.com
www.chank.com
www.fonthead.com
www.girlswhowearglasses.com
www.houseind.com
www.larabiefonts.com

PROJECT 112

Name your company

Choose a name for your production company, for example Seat of Your Pants Productions (above). Search the Internet and your local or state yellow pages to make sure that there isn't a company with that name already in existence. Design a logo and business card for your new company.

PROJECT 113

Play with type styles

Create typographic styles for the titles for four different genres of film, such as: sci-fi, horror, romantic comedy, police drama. When creating the titles, bear in mind that the title logotype will have to be used in your publicity material. Devise a teaser poster around the film's title logotype.

PROJECT 114

Make a title for your movie

Use each of the three methods (in-camera, the Saul Bass method, and the graphic design method) to make titles for your movie. For the Saul Bass method, storyboard the opening sequence.

Marketing & Publicity

Here's a little secret about the film industry: You've just made a film. People do not watch films. They watch movies. Marketing and publicity is the process that can turn your film into a movie. And here's a lie from Hollywood: They are not a filmmaking industry, they are a marketing industry, specializing in ways to turn 50 cents of blank media or plastic into a shiny box you will pay $15–$20 for.

The secret is to understand how you can create interest in your film without resorting to expensive advertising (that you can't afford) using the tool of publicity. With the right publicity you can turn your movie into this year's cult classic.

The seven essentials of creating a press kit

The people who buy movies for theaters, television, and DVD will not buy films. They only buy movies. When you have finished shooting and editing, you have a film. Now you must turn your film into a movie. The essential tool for this is a press kit.

See also:
Distribution, page 114

Filmmaking is a business. Business is about money. You will make money only if you license your film to someone to play in theaters, on DVD, on TV, or on the Internet.

A press kit is the printed material you send to a journalist or film buyer along with the DVD of your finished film. It is the way you attract attention to your movie and yourself. Hopefully the attention will also attract an acquisitions executive (film buyer).

Sample synopsis

This synopsis works because it identifies the main characters, setting, goal, and conflicts, and teases with hints of the ending, It also explains a little about the production.

The seven essentials of a successful press kit are:

1 Buy a folder

This should have two pockets inside. Print the name of your film, or film company, on the cover. Get this done by a professional; do NOT use sticky labels. Use this folder to house your documents.

2 Write a synopsis

A good synopsis is one page long, double-spaced. The last quarter of the page should be a production note.

The trick to writing a great synopsis is to give readers enough information to hook them and make them want to see more. Don't write: This happens, this happens, and then that happens. Do write: A single paragraph that would fit on the back of a DVD cover—the paragraph that hooks you into the story and makes you want to see the movie. Don't be cute or coy. If you write "Does she pull the trigger or not? You'll have to watch the film to find out," it will just irritate people. Do write the emotion. Create a word picture so that readers can start to see the movie.

VAMPIRES & OTHER STEREOTYPES

As darkness sweeps across the Big Apple, Ivan and Harry begin their night patrol. Their mission: to investigate a particularly gruesome case. But tonight they will confront an EVIL so powerful they will need more than guns to survive.

What should have been a simple operation becomes complicated by the appearance of Kirsten and her party-hopping girlfriends, who have unwittingly opened a gateway to Hell. As they try to figure out their next move, they must confront giant mutant rats, monstrous insect creatures, and a demon in their midst. Not only do they have to escape, they must figure out what these hellspawn are up to next. The clock is running out and no one knows who will make it out alive...or DEAD!

This independent production, which took two years for an extremely dedicated crew to complete, features many up-and-coming New York City actors and provides a unique twist to the genre.

Write a synopsis

PROJECT 115

Write a synopsis for your movie. Get a sheet of paper and sum up the story by completing the information below:

- **My story is about:**
  Describe the occupation of the main character.

- **Who:**
  Tell us what he or she wants more than anything else in the world.

- **But:**
  Describe the main obstacle or reason why the main character can't get what he or she wants.

- **And:**
  Tell us the outcome or ending.

3 Write biographies for the key cast and crew

The biographies should be brief, no more than three to four lines.

Draw up a list of biographies

PROJECT 116

Take a sheet of paper and head it "Key Cast and Crew Biographies." List the first and last name of every person who helped you on the film. After their names put their job title or character part. Then list the following:

1 Previous film experience. If none, write "debut." If an actor has previous stage acting experience, write: "Has worked in fringe theater on [list the productions]."
2 Relevant awards or prizes.
3 Any famous person they have worked with. If they helped out running packages for the production company of *The Dark Knight*, for example, you could write: "Has worked with Christopher Nolan."

ELLIOT GROVE, PRODUCER.
Elliot has worked on many independent films in the UK, and founded the Raindance Film Festival and the British Independent Film Awards. He was awarded an Honorary Doctorate by Britain's Open University, the largest university in the world.

BOB BINGLY, ACTOR
Bob starred in several amateur stage productions before launching his screen career with this film.

4 Draw up a list of FAQs

The FAQ technique is probably the best way to get your ideas across. Although it is not an interview, it will look like one. Successful filmmakers have used this technique to launch their careers. Quentin Tarantino wrote his own press kit for *Reservoir Dogs*, and ended each answer with a comment along the lines of: "…because Quentin Tarantino is the most creative and dynamic film director ever in the history of American cinema."

FAQs enable journalists to "fake" interviews. Often you will read "Speaking today from London, Elliot Grove said…" when what the journalist has done is read the FAQs that were mailed out.

FAQs are useful in the pre-interview before a radio or television interview. A producer will meet you in the green room and ask you questions based on your FAQs to see which ones elicit the strongest response.

Write the Q&A sheet for your movie

PROJECT 117

Title a piece of paper: The Ten Most Commonly Asked Questions of [your name] during the making of [title of your film]. These will be the questions that everyone will have been asking you from the minute you announced you wanted to make a film. Questions like: What made you give up the day job? What would you do differently if you had to do it over? After each of the questions, write the answer in no more than three or four lines. Some sample questions are listed below.

- What is the number one reason why you wanted to make this film?

- What is your background as a director/producer?

- Who are your influences as a director?

- What was the most challenging aspect of the production?

- What was the "most fun" aspect of making this movie?

- How did you go about getting the film "off the ground"?

- How long did it take to make the movie, from pre-production to final cut?

- What is the main thing you want to get across to the viewers?

- How did you go about casting the roles and getting your crew?

- What do you hope happens with the movie?

- What's next?

Press pack

Whether you are sending your movie to a film festival, production company, or distributor you should include, along with a DVD, a press release, some postcards, a poster, and film stills, preferably in digital format on a CD. The example used shows some of the publicity material for an award-winning short film called *Broken*.

5 Organize publicity photographs

To market and promote your film, you will need good photographs of you and of your cast. A mug shot might be acceptable for your high school yearbook, but it will not be selected by magazine picture editors. If you want to have pictures on posters, DVD jackets, websites, and in magazine articles, you should take photographs during production. Action pictures are best.

Get the cast to reenact key moments of the shoot. It's not a good idea to take publicity pictures during filming because your photographer might distract the actors, or the shutter might get picked up on the sound track. Arrange for a stills photographer to attend on the days when you have the most equipment and the most people working on set so they can photograph cast and crew.

6 Build a website

Filmmakers can use a website to take and receive messages, as a gallery for photographs and trailers, and to put vital press kit elements online so that film journalists, film festival programmers, film buyers, and anyone else can easily access vital information.

7 Get reviewed and interviewed

Press reviews will start to turn your film into a movie. Film journalists most likely start working on a free weekly community newspaper and get to do the entertainment page, based on the press kits of the films playing at the multiplex. They are probably allowed a couple of hours to pull this together. Your press kit is key to getting a mention. Any review is better than no review. You can nearly always extract a positive phrase or even a word to hype your movie.

The basics of building a website

Domain name
Try to come up with a domain name that is close to the name of your film. Then register it.

Plan your website
Decide the different levels of the website on paper. By making it work on paper you can make it work online.

About Us

Home page

Film portfolio

Start a video diary
Ask your actors to answer key questions about the making of the film during the shoot and tape them. The answers should be rhetorical in form. You can publish them on your website if you wish. These interviews will become part of the DVD extras.

Make a picture gallery
Put thumbnails of the best pictures online so they will load quickly, but make it clear to visitors that they can get a hi-res image by double-clicking.

Look at other similar websites
Visit these websites created by first-time filmmakers:

- *www.blairwitchproject.com*
- *www.otnemem.com* (the website for Christopher Nolan's *Memento*)

Now plan a website for your movie.

Start a newsletter
It doesn't need to be massive; just monthly updates of where you are with the film. It will enable the production, cast, crew, and investors to keep up to date with the progress of the film during production. Once your film is finished, film festivals and film buyers can get a sense of how your film is doing.

Get blogging
Start a blog on your website. A blog is easy to set up and it is a great way to keep track of things that happen during the making of your film. It's very easy to forget key moments; a blog will help you capture them. You can decide later whether or not you want your blog to be public.

e-News
Create the newsletter on your website or blog, then e-mail the URL to everyone on your mailing list. Remember to put all their names in BCC (blind carbon copy).

Update: April 2009

- The principal two-week shooting was completed last week, with additional pick-ups (special effects) scheduled for later this month.

- Editing is scheduled to begin within three weeks in order to keep on schedule for a rough-cut by spring.

- Additional CGI effects will be done during editing.

About film festivals

A film festival is an organized series of film screenings over an extended period of time. A festival's job is to deliver an audience of enthusiasts eager to see each film featured.

See also:
How to start your own film festival, page 110

Film festivals are more popular than ever. Distributors use festivals to create awareness of their smaller and artier films. Festivals bring filmmakers and interested audiences together.

Some festivals specialize in a particular theme or genre (horror movies or documentaries), while many cater to independent films that express certain ideological or cultural viewpoints. The Tribeca Film Festival was started by Robert De Niro to rebuild confidence in New York following the terror attacks of 9/11; it has been a contributing factor in restoring that city's tourist appeal.

Well-known festivals such as Cannes (France), Sundance (United States), and Raindance (United Kingdom) have a huge influence on the movie industry, especially in shaping critical expectations.

Must-see sites

■ **www.withoutabox.com** is part of the Amazon/IMDb group. The website handles online submissions to a majority of the world's film festivals and can be searched by specific criteria such as genre and location.

■ **www.filmfestivalworld.com** lists upcoming festivals and submission deadlines by date, location, and genre, giving detailed information about each festival and links to their websites.

■ **www.filmandfestivals.com** is an independent digital magazine that reports on film festivals and profiles new, upcoming, and established filmmakers.

Festival types

Festivals are categorized according to the number of industry people who attend them—film buyers, financiers, agents, producers, actors, writers, and technicians.

Major

There are 20 major film festivals defined as Category One by the International Federation of Film Producers Associations (FIAPF). The top five film festivals in the world are: Cannes, Toronto, Sundance, Berlin, and Rotterdam.

The Cannes Film Festival is the largest in the world. Held annually in Cannes, France, the festival is attended by over 6,500 industry professionals, as well as by another 35,000–40,000 film lovers and wannabees.

To have your film selected by a major film festival is one way to qualify it for an Oscar nomination. The other way is to rent (called four wall) a theater in Los Angeles County during the calendar year.

Mini-major

Mini-majors are also important, but have fewer industry personnel attending than major film festivals. Festivals like Telluride, Palm Springs, Deauville, Tribeca, and Raindance fall into this category.

City

City film festivals are funded solely by civic fathers to promote the sense of culture in the city. Examples of such festivals include New York, Edinburgh, London, Venice, Rome, and Chicago.

Genre

You will often see festivals with words like Sci-fi, Frightfest, Fantasy, Horror, Animation, Shorts, and Gay and Lesbian in the title. This refers to the genre the festival specializes in and is known for. Only specialist distribution companies send their film buyers to these festivals. If you have a genre film, these festivals are certainly well worth attending.

Some festivals are created by private individuals to celebrate their own particular interests. Paris has at least two Woody Allen film festivals, and there are hundreds of specialized film festivals all over the world where the festival organizers play the types of films that they want to see. These festivals are generally very small and are seldom attended by film buyers. They do, however, provide an interesting cultural texture to the cities where they are held.

SCI-FI-LONDON
The UK's premiere genre film festival dedicated to showing independent science fiction films that won't be showing at your local multiplex.

Cannes crowd
Notice the different attire on Cannes' red carpet: tuxedos, business suits, and casual wear. The largest film festival in the world attracts film lovers of all levels.

The culture test

When researching a film festival, it is useful to try and see where the festival features on the cultural map of the city that hosts it. Research and answer the following questions about your nearest city. Does it have:

- **A symphony orchestra?** What is it called?

- **An opera company?** What is it called?

- **A ballet company?** What is it called?

- **A museum?** What is it called?

- **A public art gallery?** What is it called?

- **A film festival?** If so, what is it called?

Film festivals are often funded by civic authorities to help promote tourism and sell hotel accommodation and meals in local restaurants. Now look into the details of the festival and make a note of your research (see right).

- **Does the festival have a website?**

- **What are the dates of the festival?**

- **What is its submissions policy?**

Keep a record
Using a computer database, or old-fashioned index cards, keep a record of film festivals you research or want to submit to.

- ■ **Festival:** *The Times BFI London Film Festival*
- ■ **Date:** *14–29 October*
- ■ **Submission Policy:**
  - *DVD copy of the film*
  - *synopsis and/or press kit.*
- ■ **Awards:** *Best Fiction Feature Film; Best Documentary; Best Short Film; Best Student Film; Best Creative Documentary...*

- ■ **Festival:** *The London Greek Film Festival*
- ■ **Date:** *13–16 November*
- ■ **Submission Policy:**
  - *DVD copy of the film*
  - *synopsis and/or press kit.*
- ■ **Awards:** *Best Short Film; Best Documentary; Best Animation; Best Student Film; Best Director.*

How to start your own film festival

Anyone can start a film festival. Go to the best movie theater in town and ask to see the manager. Tell the manager that you want to rent a screen for your film festival. The manager will then negotiate a rental charge, including the cost of projectionists and theater ushers.

See also:
About film festivals, page 108

There are seven key elements to running a film festival.

1 Mission statement

Before you start a film festival, you need to decide what it is that will make your film festival unique. With more than 4,000 film festivals around the world, your festival needs to be distinctive. It also needs to be something that you feel really passionate about, for how else are you going to be able to motivate yourself for all the long hours it will take to organize and run a festival.

2 Programing

Develop a network with sales agents, local distributors, other film festivals, and filmmakers to make sure that you have a great flow of excellent films coming your way to choose from. You will also want to schedule some of the following elements into your festival:

- **Parties**—where audience members can network and meet filmmakers.
- **Film focus**—where you choose cinema from a country or region that has been previously neglected.
- **Honor and tributes**—where you single out a filmmaker of repute and invite him or her to give a talk followed by a retrospective screening of his or her favorite film.
- **Events and training**—where filmmakers and audiences alike can get up to speed with the latest developments.
- **The very best films of the genre or type that you want to show**, be it horror, or shorts, or movies shot on cell phones—whatever type of film and cinema that excites you.

3 Timeline

Next, you want to get a rough idea of what your timeline is, along with key milestones and targets:

- **Month 1**
  - Prepare mission statement
- **Months 1–6**
  - Create budget
  - Secure sponsorship
- **Months 6–9**
  - Call for submissions
- **Months 9–10**
  - Watch submissions and choose lineup
- **Month 11**
  - Festival press launch
  - Initiate marketing campaign
  - First volunteers' meeting
- **Month 12**
  - Assemble all the screening prints
  - Prepare hospitality for visiting filmmakers
  - Final event planning
  - Opening night gala

4 Budget

Once you have an idea of the events and films you want to show, you will need to prepare a budget.

PROJECT 126

Make your festival budget

Draw up a budget to present to potential sponsors and funding bodies using the list on the right as a guide. It is much better to overestimate than underestimate; overestimating gives you an advantage when negotiating.

FESTIVAL BUDGET

Cash: In kind

Venue: Local cinema

Advertising:
- Local radio
- Google awards
- Local newspaper ads

Marketing:
- Leaflets & postcards
- Posters
- T-shirts

Publicity:
- Press agent

Expenses:
- Opening night party
- Drinks
- Goody bags

Staffing:
- Festival director
- Assistant
- Designer

TOTAL EXPENDITURE:

Income:
- Box office
- Sale of tees & other merchandise
- Sponsorship

TOTAL INCOME:

Profit/Loss:

THE 16TH RAINDANCE FILM FESTIVAL

1–12 OCTOBER 2008

You should get out more

See the very best independent film from the UK and around the world

Details www.raindance.co.uk

Festival program

The festival program should have an enticing image on the cover, usually relating to the poster, along with the festival's branding/logo. It should contain short but positive reviews of the films, with at least one still photo, along with a detailed list of screening times.

6 Submissions

Once you have your mission statement and your budget in place you will want to issue a call for submissions in order to attract films to your film festival. At this point you should consider whether you are willing to offer prizes to attract films. If so, how will you select your jury and how are the awards going to be chosen?

7 Press release

The first paragraph should clearly state where and when your festival is and what the submission deadline is. You should also state any special restrictions, such as completion date, topic, and length.

The second paragraph should restate the festival mission statement, and list prizes and how they are selected.

After the end of the press release, you can include notes to the editor in which you thank sponsors or remind journalists about the history of the event.

You will get a lot more news coverage if you can get a celebrity to allow you to quote him or her in the press release, saying something very positive about your festival.

Once you have a press release, you need to distribute it. Sometimes it will pay to advertise your festival submissions on websites like *www.filmfestivals.com*, *www.withoutabox.com*, and *www.indiewire.com*. Other websites like *www.shootingpeople.org* do not charge for submissions, but there is a modest annual subscription fee before you can post. It is also a great idea to research film schools and film organizations and send the press release to them. Remember that there are hundreds of these outside the United States as well as inside. The catch phrase for a film festival is "think global."

5 Schedule

If your festival runs for one week, you will most likely run for a "theatrical week" from Friday until Thursday. New films open on a Friday and run for a week, and so this is an easier slot for the theater to rent to you; it is difficult for them to rent a half week to a distributor. If you plan to open with a big gala followed by a party at a nearby club, it might prove to be difficult to find a club that is available on a Friday night. If so, go back to the theater owner and see if they will rent you a slot on Thursday. Whatever the length of your festival, you will then have to make a schedule. Here's a sample schedule:

	FRI	SAT	SUN	MON	TUES	WED	THURS
10am			(2)	(2)		(7)	
12pm			(2)	(2)			
2pm							
4pm				(3)	(3)	(3)	(3)
6pm		(5)	(5)	(5)	(5)	(4)	(5)
8pm	(1)				(4)		(8)
10pm							
12am		(6)	(6)				

KEY: (1) Opening night gala followed by a party; (2) Seminars and workshops; (3) Film focus; (4) Tribute and screening; (5) Short film screenings; (6) Midnight madness slots; (7) Your film screening; (8) Closing night gala

PROJECT 127

Create a schedule

Use the form on the left as a template to draw up your own film festival schedule.

Film markets

Where film festivals are about glitz, glamor, red carpets, and stars, film markets are rather cold and impersonal— and dedicated solely to the buying and selling of films. Successful filmmakers understand how film markets

There are thousands of film festivals around the world, but only three film markets:

- **February:** Berlin, European Film Market
- **May:** Cannes, Marché du Film (Cannes Film Market)
- **November:** Los Angeles, American Film Market

There is a small market for indie films each September in New York City called the Independent Feature Film Market (IFFM).

How film markets work
Each film market has a market organizer that rents an exhibition space and sublets stalls or booths to interested vendors. On the days of the actual market, security guards make sure that only qualified people attend: film buyers, film sellers, and accredited personnel. These people could be employees of one of the companies attending the market, or industry professionals according to the mandate of the particular market.

In 2008, for example, more than 350 film buyers from Japan attended the Cannes Film Market. One buyer was on his own looking for product to sell in his chain of three home video stores on the northern island; while Gaga Entertainment, one of the largest distributors in Japan, had more than two dozen employees at Cannes. Both companies were attending the film markets looking for films, and both companies had checkbooks. So, if it is so simple, why don't more filmmakers attend film markets and sell direct to the film buyers? The answer, like many things in life, is money. You can't just show up at EFM, Cannes, or AFM and start selling your films; you need to be accredited. This means that you need to join the market. Each market has different fees. Plus you need to fly staff to the market and accommodate them. In addition, you need to rent booth space in the market exhibition areas. And lastly, you need to advertise to the film buyers that you are at the market with your film.

People say that you need a minimum of $50,000 to attend a market. And you won't have that money if you have finished your film. In fact, you will be down and out. The solution is to employ a film sales agent.

Three types of films are sold at film markets: finished films, films halfway through production, and films that are at script stage, called either "In Development" or in "Pre-Production."

Film sales agents
A sales agent who specializes in selling film is called a film sales agent. Many specialize

WALKING BETWEEN THE RAINDROPS

Stanley meets Sarah at a party. They begin casually spending time together as they juggle their responsibilities as college students in Southern California. Stanley is a film major and Sarah a psychology major. Their different career interests and values make for some very interesting and humorous conversations, which not only effectively highlight their unique personalities but also some of the major differences between men and women.

Told from Stanley's point of view, the film steadily draws the viewer into Stanley's world and his developing feelings toward Sarah. As Stanley and Sarah spend more and more time together, Stanley discovers that he has fallen in love with her—and believes he has found "the one." But does Sarah feel the same?

Examples of "one-sheets"
A one-sheet is a letter-sized graphic poster with two sides: one displaying a title, graphic, and tag line; the other offering a summary. These examples show the kind of text suitable for a one-sheet.

WEREWOLF TALES

With the power of the beast comes the hunger, a hunger that cannot always be controlled. Here are the stories of three men whose lives are changed by the caprice of lycanthropy. There's the mob boss who is cursed by an ancient evil, a nebbish man who craves power he's never had and will do anything to get, and the descendent of a certain Dr. Jekyll, who has reconstituted the formula created by his great grandfather... These are...Werewolf Tales!

---

in different genres, such as action, art house, horror, documentaries, and shorts. Sometimes an agent may agree to represent at script stage, although this is not common for first-time directors.

An agent:
- promotes the film at film markets and major film festivals;
- negotiates the deal terms with distributors;
- makes sure the filmmaker delivers all the elements of the sold films, including a release print, the inter-negative and inter-positives, sound masters, the script, and any legal documents;
- provides regular financial accounts for client filmmakers, including a breakdown of costs and income for each film.

Agents charge a commission, which varies according to the amount of work the filmmaker needs them to do. If the press kit is not finished, the music is not cleared, or key artwork for posters and DVD jackets is not done, the agent can take over but the sales commission will rise accordingly. The money paid out by the agent is recouped from the first money in.

The agent's main promotional tools are trailers and a double-sided leaflet called the one-sheet.

Trailers and one-sheets

A good trailer is short (two to three minutes), captures the emotion of the movie, and entices the viewer to see more. However, a trailer cut by a sales agent is intended to give a distributor a quick overview of the story and an idea of the type of film, so it will largely consist of the

scenes with the most action and is put together on a minimal budget. If you are trying to raise finance for your film, it may pay you to create a mood and ambience piece, with higher production values, that is more likely to impress a potential investor.

The front of a one-sheet comprises a cover image with a strong graphic that sums up the type of film, the title of the film, and a one-line summary, called the log line.

On the reverse is a short paragraph that outlines the story, followed by a paragraph that sums up the main attributes of the filmmaker. There should be a second powerful image from the film, along with the credits and contact details.

Distribution

A film distributor is a company or individual who acts as the intermediary between a filmmaker (or the sales agent) and a theater owner (known as the exhibitor). Film distribution refers to the marketing and promotion of movies in theaters and home entertainment (DVD, downloads, television).

See also:
Movies on the Internet, page 115

Once you have secured a distributor for a territory, they will need to convince local exhibitors to schedule your film into their theater. The exhibitor's main agenda is to decide whether or not money can be made from the screening.

The distributor's role

- Attempts to persuade the exhibitor by screening the film and then demonstrating the planned marketing and publicity campaigns.
- Signs an agreement with the exhibitor, stipulating the amount of the gross ticket sales to be paid to the distributor.
- Makes sure that enough film prints are struck and delivered to each theater, along with marketing materials.
- Designs and books ads in newspapers, magazines, websites, and radio stations.
- Submits the film to local censorship bodies.

- Secures dubbing or subtitling for foreign language editions of the film
- Monitors the exhibitors on opening day to make sure the film is being screened at the agreed times and venues.
- Ensures that the exhibitors e-mail them the box office reports.
- Manages the release windows, and decides when the film should be released for television and home entertainment.
- Pays the filmmaker a flat fee to cover all the income from the territory the distributor controls, or a percentage of the distributor's profit.

More than 90 percent of all films released in theaters lose money. If this is the case, why do distributors bother to release films in theaters? Because when the general public sees the ads for a movie in the theater, as well as reviews in newspapers

and magazines, they assume that the film is worth paying money to see. If they do not go to the theater to see the movie, they are much more likely to rent or buy it on a DVD, or pay a premium to see it on a cable TV channel like HBO and Showtime (United States), Rogers (Canada), or Sky Plus (UK).

This means that showing a movie in a theater increases the value of the other windows many times more than for a non-theatrical release.

Unfortunately for an independent filmmaker, it is very difficult to get a movie released in theaters, unless there are named actors attached. Even then, a film made independently has an uphill battle to get into theaters. Another route is to self-distribute or get your movie on the Internet.

Reality check

Here is a typical theatrical release: Let's suppose your film took $1,000,000 from theaters. Here is where the money goes. Further deductions can include the cost of transferring a digital print to film, the cost of clearing music, preparing marketing materials, and so on.

		$	$
Income from theater ticket sales			1,000,000
Less	Exhibitor's share (50%)	500,000	165,000
	Distributor's share (33%)	(665,000)	
			335,000
Less	Prints and Advertising (P&A budget)		
	prints ($2,000 per print x 100 cinemas)	200,000	
	advertising	200,000	
	publicity	20,000	
		(420,000)	
			-85,000
TOTAL THEATRICAL PROFIT			**-$85,000**

Movies on the Internet

On February 15, 2005, three former Paypal employees started www.youtube.com, marking the start of a revolutionary way of watching movies on the Internet and creating a new frontier of distribution possibilities for independent filmmakers.

During an interview in 1968, film director Jean-Luc Goddard said: "We must find new ways of making films and especially new ways of showing them... If we know something of movies because we have worked in them for several years, maybe we can tell people about it so that they can invent the television or movie they need. Up until now they didn't know that they needed one. Very often they are glad for the television. They don't even think that they could or that people should speak on TV to each other."

A 21st-century solution

YouTube demonstrated that it was possible to have a uniform interface system on the Internet that would allow people using different types of computers to watch movies formatted on different types of cameras. The YouTube website grew tremendously fast—within six months of its launch, more than 65,000 video clips a day were being uploaded onto it.

Filmmakers started creating short pieces specifically for the new Web audience. Videos like *Charlie the Unicorn*, characters like Old Gregg, and video sites like HellfireComms became overnight successes with millions of viewers.

Internet Protocol Television (IPTV) is the next generation of film distribution. The advances made in this media field since 2007 have been staggering.

What is an IPTV platform?

There are three main types of IPTV platform: ad-based, pay-per-views, and cell phones. IPTV platforms cover live TV (multicasting) as well as stored video (Video on Demand—VOD). Multicasting is used to send information to multiple computers at the same time.

IP platforms offer many advantages, including the ability to integrate television with other IP-based services like high speed Internet, the delivery of significantly more content and functionality, and opportunities to make the viewing experience more interactive and personalized.

How are films shown on the Internet?

Since 2007, websites like *Joost.com, Vimeo.com, Blinkx.com, Babelgum. com*, and *Raindance.tv* have pioneered assembling and showing films and TV shows on the Internet. Films are presented in two ways—streaming or download. A download infers that the file for the film is transferred onto a home computer and then watched at home. With streaming, if

YouTube
By far the most popular host for viral videos, YouTube provides an outlet for anyone to upload family vacation footage, professional films, and everything in between.

Babelgum

Babelgum is an ad-funded Internet platform that streams professionally produced, TV-quality shows and videos. Editorially focused on indie films, this site hosts the Babelgum Online Film Festival.

Raindance.tv

An ad-free film port, *Raindance.tv* streams high-quality shorts, features, and documentaries made by independent filmmakers.

you want to watch a movie, you need to be connected to the Internet. Portions of the film are fed to your computer or "streamed," allowing you to watch the movie for as long as you are connected.

How can filmmakers make money on the Internet?

There are three different ways that filmmakers can earn money from having their movies streamed or downloaded.

Pay Per View (PPV) requires the viewer to pay a sum for the right to see the film. Sometimes the fee is similar to that of renting a DVD, and sometimes it is equivalent to the price of buying a DVD.

Watching ads is the second and more popular method. It requires the viewer to agree to watch the ads, which can be imbedded before and after the film (pre-roll and end roll). Part of the ad revenue is deducted by the website hosting the film to cover the cost of transmission, and part is shared (called ad rev) with the filmmaker.

Sponsorship is when a brand commissions or pays to host a series of films. Part of the sponsorship money can be paid to participating filmmakers and part is used to cover the costs of transmission.

blinkx.com

Blinkx is a search engine specially designed for video and audio content. Special speech recognition software allows search queries to pull dialogue directly from the audio of online films.

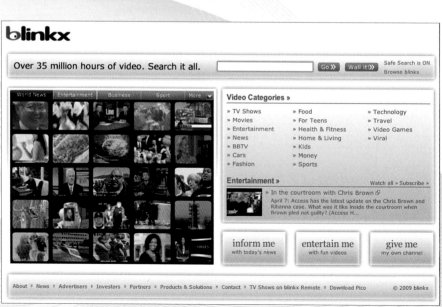

Getting your work online

Sign up to film-sharing social-networking site Vimeo simply by registering your name, e-mail address, and password, and agreeing to the terms and conditions. Once you're a part of the community, you can press Upload in the upper right-hand corner of your screen. Then, select your movie from its location on your computer. Enter your movie's title and a short synopsis, so people know what they'll be watching. Add appropriate tag words (see project 129 below). From here, you can take control of who watches your movie. Think about what kind of audience you want—do you want only your friends to see your film? Or as many people as possible? What Vimeo channels do you want your film associated with?

Signing up
Vimeo's simple graphical interface makes it easy to sign up for an account.

Tagging your movie

People will find your movies in one or two ways—through word of mouth or by stumbling across it after entering search words into Internet search engines. You will notice that on Vimeo, you can tag your film. Go onto eBay or Google and look for the 100 most searched keywords. Of those lists, figure out which ones you can incorporate with your film. Tagging with hot key words and phrases makes your film more searchable and yields better search results.

Looking for love
Tags help people find your film. If it is tagged with the word "love," the search results will put your film in the list, which are usually sorted by popularity. Searches will also show other tags related to the main search.

Rights

In simple terms, you own the copyright to any original work that you create, unless and until you sign those rights over to another person or organization. It's then that the whole issue of rights becomes murky and filled with lots of legalities and jargon that seem mainly to benefit the lawyers.

Check these out

www.creativecommons.org
Advice on copyright and sharing your work. Especially relevant for the Internet.

www.raindance.co.uk
Home of the Raindance Festival and courses and services for filmmakers, including script registration

www.wga.org
Writers Guild of America for registering screenplays

Clearance and Copyright
Michael C. Donaldson (Silman-James Press (2nd ed.), 2003)

Getting Permission: How to License and Clear Copyrighted Materials Online and Off
Richard Stim (Nolo Press, 2000)

www.opensourcecinema.org:
An excellent documentary about copyright in the digital world.

You may not need to prove or defend the originality of your work while it remains in the non profit realm of private showings, but the sooner you learn to protect yourself, the better. This starts at the script-writing stage and usually involves registering your script with an organization such as the Writers' Guild of America (WGA; *www.wga.org*) or a similar local organization. There is usually a fee for this, and it can be done on the Internet. The chance that a story similar to your original idea already exists is high, but having your screenplay registered is still your best protection.

Of course, if your screenplay is for your own episode of *Star Wars*, you may have trouble registering it. That doesn't stop you from making it as a fan film; you just can't sell it or make money from it—unless of course George Lucas gives his permission and blessing.

Material protected under copyright can go beyond identifiable characters to include any recognizable product, work of art, or piece of music. Different countries have different rules, but it is best to abide by international copyright law, just to be on the safe side. We live in extremely litigious times, and a slight oversight in getting proper clearances could hinder the release of your breakout film for years, with the lawyers being the only ones making money. If you are going to have well-known products in your shots, get permission from the copyright owners or the manufacturers before you start shooting.

If you are clever, you should be able to turn it to your advantage, particularly if there is another major competitive brand. If your star needs to drink a can of cola, you can approach your preferred brand and ask them not only to supply the permission but also all the cans necessary for the shoot. Product placement is big business, so why not get a slice of that action and cover yourself at the same time?

The use of music has been covered on pages 96–99, but be aware that any songs playing on a radio or stereo in the scene are still classified as a performance, and will need (expensive) clearance. By now you will know not to have such electronic devices on during filming anyway, simply as a continuity issue; they are added in post-production.

For your first attempts at making films, it is probably best not to worry too much about eliminating all branding from the shoot, as it is unlikely to be seen by the general public. However, if your talent and/or ambition are so great that you are confident of the work being shown in

Watch out!
This type of wording simply means you are signing your work away, so you'd better hope they are paying you well.

Read the small print
"I hereby irrevocably and unconditionally waive any so-called 'moral rights of authors' in the Programs and such rights under section 106 of the Copyright Act of 1976 as I now have or hereafter acquire in relation to the Programs."

public, then it is best to do the right thing from the start. You might be able to claim "fair usage," especially on not-for-profit (as opposed to not profitable) movies, in the sense that the items are in common use in everyday life, and provided they are not an integral part of the story, you will probably be safe, although restricted in where you can show the finished film.

The whole subject of copyright is complex and fills many large and very dull books. If you have doubts, seek legal advice; it may save you a lot of money and aggravation in the long run. That goes for any contracts or agreements you are asked to sign as well. Distributors are out to make money above anything else, and even if you assign all the rights to them, you can be pretty sure

that if litigation results from your oversight, they will send the lawyers to you. Bear that in mind before you sign away the rights to your work. Always err on the side of caution, and remember that even if it is a lo-no budget film, the law does not look on poverty as a defense.

Check your rights

When submitting your film to a festival, competition, website, or for broadcast, always read the terms and conditions very carefully before you sign anything. Most are there to protect your rights and intellectual property, but some may use clever wording that turns your rights over to them. If in doubt, seek legal advice.

TYPICAL CONTRACT (FOR FESTIVAL ENTRANCE)

By submitting an Entry, you hereby (a) represent that you are the sole author and owner of your Entry and your Entry is under no restriction, contractual or otherwise, which will prevent The Festival's use of it or you from meeting your obligations; (b) agree that the Entry shall be free of all liens, encumbrances, and claims of third parties; (c) acknowledge and agree that nothing in your Entry infringes on any copyrights or trademarks, or violates any person's rights of privacy or publicity and that you have obtained all necessary releases and permissions; and (d) agree to comply with these official rules and the terms of service.

Entries determined by The Festival to infringe on any intellectual property rights, or other rights, will be disqualified and no refunds will be given. All materials submitted become property of The Festival (but not the intellectual property rights, as described below).

RIGHTS: As part of the entry process, you must execute the official Submission Agreement. Please review this Submission Agreement carefully! By executing the Submission Agreement, you will be, among other things, promising that you have obtained all necessary rights and clearances in connection with your film.

If your film is chosen as a finalist, The Festival will have the non-exclusive right to exploit your film in any way, in its sole discretion (but not the obligation to exploit your film in any way). In addition, derivative rights to your film will be licensed to The Festival for a minimum period of two years, as set forth in the Submission Agreement.

If you do not obtain all rights and fully complete the Submission Agreement, your film will not be considered for entry.

This refers to the physical medium the film was sent on, not the movie itself.

"Non-exclusive" is a very important term as it allows you to show it at other places.

Two years is a fairly standard length of time for a festival to use your work, although it doesn't state a maximum period. Remember, if you are at this stage, your work is being promoted at no expense to yourself—so it is a small price to pay.

Writing a good résumé

Your résumé is the quickest way of telling a potential employer who you are and what you can do. Keep it brief, because most employers are too busy to read lots of pages. And don't be too "creative" with your experiences, because everybody knows everybody in the film industry.

A résumé is an essential tool for selling yourself. You should include:

Name/Heading
At the top of your résumé should be your full name and contact information. You may want to include an e-mail address as well as a personal cell phone number.

Objective
Begin your résumé with a summary of your background and collective knowledge. While you want to be descriptive of your experience, it is important to be concise. Essentially, you want to "hook" your prospective employer with your objective. Your credentials are as important as the way in which you write them. Pay strict attention to grammar and mechanics, but particularly to structure. It is important for your sentences to be sophisticated and fluid, yet easily readable.

Education
Detail your education in a series of bullets. Include the name of your school, the degree(s) you have earned, any graduating honors, and any relevant coursework. You may also want to provide a brief description of some courses, as well as the topic of your thesis project.

Relevant coursework
List any film-related coursework, highlighting specific areas you have studied, such as film theory, lighting, editing, sound or film directing, and producing.
Then list additional coursework or training, highlighting all the software you have been trained to use, such as Final Cut Pro, AfterEffects, InDesign, Shake, Combustion.

Relevant experience
Detail the experience you have had within your field of study in a series of bullets. List any paid or voluntary jobs and include the dates during which you worked. Instead of listing your responsibilities, focus on what you accomplished in a brief summary. Include your proficiency with relevant software programs, computer systems, etc.

Activities
This is an opportunity for you to include any accomplishments that are relevant to your field of interest. These can be membership in academic clubs or organizations, awards or honors earned, or personal interests.

Special interests
Employers are very interested in your hobbies and special interests. It is from this section that they get an idea of your "taste."

PROJECT 130

Write your own résumé
Decide on the job you would really like to have. Write a résumé to submit. For example:

Objective
Clearly state what your ideal position or career would be. Don't say: "To win an Oscar"; instead, say "to become an editor's assistant" (achievable and quantifiable).

Work experience
Latest employer, city (date), title
• *roles you fulfilled or projects worked on*

Activities
List any special interests where you were members of formal clubs, groups, societies, etc.

● Susannah Miles

96 Manhattan Blvd.
New York, NY 60245
Email: susiem@hotmail.com
Ph: 212-555-8796

Your name

Contact details
including cell
phone and e-mail
Include the full zip code

Objective
An adaptable, determined, and self-motivated film graduate eager to become an editor's assistant, and to build upon the skills learned during my time at college.

Education
West Side College of Film and Media 2004–2007
MFA in Film Editing

Education
*Most recent school
Your degree or the
course taken
Relevant coursework
Any additional courses
or training*

Relevant Coursework
Introduction to Film
Film Theory
Lighting
Editing
Introductory Sound Editing
Film Production 1
Film Production 2

Additional Courses:
Introduction to Stop-Frame Animation
Cinematic Storytelling

Work Experience
Runner—Black and Blue Media, NYC 2008–present
Working closely with First Assistant Director to ensure the smooth running of the editing process, taking messages from editing department to the set, and delivering rushes.
Worked on: *Archangel II*, *Another Day in Hell*, and *The Taxman Cometh*.

Floor Runner—Brooklyn Film Studios, NYC 2007–2008
Conveying messages, organizing props, driving, delivering technical equipment, and attending to specific requests from the Producer, Director, or Assistant Directors. Worked on: *Junk III*, *The Miracle Cure*, and *The Return of Providence*.

Activities
Girls on Top Film Club 2006–present
Women's filmmaking club, focusing on social issues affecting the lives of young women.

"Comedy Slam" Competition (1st Place) 2006
College competition to create a 6-minute comedy film. Won 1st prize with *The Meaning of Loaf*—a bread-based investigation into the life of the modern student.

Frederick's Neighborhood Community Film Project 2005
Community project to help disadvantaged kids get involved in documentary filmmaking.

Special skills
Clean driving license
Fluent in Spanish

Hobbies and interests
Rock climbing
Baking

Special skills
*List any languages or skills, such as
computer programms, you have
mastered. Include driving license, etc.*

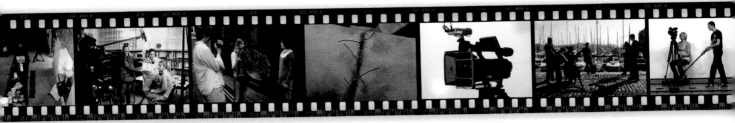

A–Z of independent filmmaking

Blondes and redheads are portable lights for film and photography that plug into a standard main socket.

A is for Actor, the most exploited component of an independent film. Actors often work for free in a feature film in the hope that it will launch their careers. Independent filmmakers often hire a name actor for a day in a cameo role in the hope that the "name" will help pull in investors and enhance sales. In the United States, the actors on low-budget independent features are called "the moveable props" due to their abundant supply.

B is for Blonde. This is the nickname for a 2k portable light that can be plugged into household current. A 750-watt light is called a redhead. These lights are considered the staple of independent filmmakers. Hence the statement, "I'm shooting with a blonde and two redheads." This equipment can be packed in a small case and easily transported with a camera in the back of a taxi.

BIFA, the acronym for the British Independent Film Awards (*http://www.bifa.org.uk*), are the only awards specifically for independently produced film in Europe.

C is for "culture jamming," a publicity technique used by many independent filmmakers as a way to enhance scanty marketing budgets by associating themselves (uninvited) with highly successful brands, or by courting controversy.

Cameras must suit the story and the budget. Film cameras are defined by the width (gauge) of the film stock: 8 mm, 16 mm, 35 mm, and 70 mm. Specialty gauges are super 8 mm, super 16 mm, and super 35 mm. Imax cameras take 70 mm film sideways to allow for a 135 mm x 70 mm frame. Tape formats are VHS, Super VHS, Beta, Digibeta, Mini DV, DVCAM, DVPro, and HDTV.

D is for Distribution, the most difficult barrier for an independent filmmaker to surmount. Filmmakers can resort to alternative distribution techniques. In Europe, more than 95 percent of the cinema screens are owned by American studios, making access to distribution even trickier.

Digital technology. This has revolutionized the filmmaking industry by lowering the financial threshold for entry to the film industry, thus making filmmaking much more democratic.

E is for Edit Decision List (EDL)—the cutting points of all the edits during the movie. Creating the EDL is the job of the editor, one of the key creatives on any filmmaking team. The editor is responsible for reordering the visual and audio material collected during the shoot to enhance the story. Inexpensive desktop editing systems, such as Apple's Final Cut Pro, have made it easier and cheaper for filmmakers to edit their material.

F is for Film Festival, which is traditionally the launchpad for independent films. Filmmakers attend in the hope of achieving either notoriety or celebrity status. They also hope to sell their film to a distributor.

"**Four wall**" is the self-distribution technique employed by filmmakers with no distribution deal or those who want to control the release of the film. They purchase all the seats in a cinema at a discount and then program their own film and resell the tickets.

G is for Grips, Gaffers, and Gophers—nicknames for various members of the crew. A grip moves or rigs anything that camera equipment attaches to (or grips) and is in charge of dollies, cranes, and special camera mounts. The first assistant is called the Key Grip. A gaffer is the chief electrician who moves and rigs lights. Gaffers are named after a hook for hanging overhead lights. The first assistant is called the Best Boy. A gopher is a runner who will "go for" anything required by the production.

Guerrilla filmmaking is the term used to describe any tactics that skirt the fringes of the law. For example, shooting in the street technically requires a permit, but guerrilla filmmakers will shoot without a permit.

H is for Helicam. In order to emulate big-budget films, indie filmmakers needing a helicopter shot often use inexpensive model helicopters fitted with small cameras and remote-control devices.

I is for Investor, the key to any film. Learning to approach an investor successfully is one of the most important "filmmaking" skills to acquire.

Indiewood is a nickname for films made on large budgets, often financed by studios, that attempt to emulate the topics and look of indie films. Examples include *Memento, Pulp Fiction*, and *Gosford Park*.

J is for Job, which is what a lot of filmmakers have to have in order to keep the wolves from the door while they are making their movie.

K is for KISS (Keep It Simple Stupid)—the basic requirement of an independent film. No children, no animals, no special effects, and minimal locations equals simple to shoot, simple to edit, and of course, simple to finance.

L is for Location, which is a cheaper option than shooting on a set. The challenge is to find a series of locations close enough for easy travel.

The steadicam allows the camera operator to follow the action without getting the distracting camera shake of handheld shooting.

Old clockwork 16 mm camera that still works as well as the day it was made.

Often scripts are written with a series of locations in mind, e.g., *El Mariachi*. The ultimate low-budget films are shot in one location in order to minimize costs, e.g., *Reservoir Dogs*, *The Blair Witch Project*, *Night of the Living Dead*, and *Shallow Grave*.

M is for mother. Even independent filmmakers get down sometimes and need a hug! M is also for money, something parents often provide. Hence the definition of independent film is "no single source financing, your mother's excepted."

N is for Negative, the most frequently used word in the film industry. Typical industry ways of saying "no" are: "I'll call you," or, "thank you for sharing that with me."

O is for Oscar, the Hollywood equivalent of knighthood. The top indie awards are the Spirit Awards and the British Independent Film Awards.

P is for Passion, the one thing that distinguishes independent film: passionate stories made by passionate people. You have to have a lot of passion to get your movie made.

Q is for Queer Cinema, often on the cutting edge of cinema. Filmmakers like Greg Araki (*Totally F**ked Up*) and Percy Adlon (*Bagdad Cafe, My Own Private Idaho*) helped expand the narrative storytelling horizon.

R is for Rejection. Successful filmmakers must learn how to handle heaps of rejection. It usually starts with friends and family saying, "Why don't you get a real job."

S is for Script, the most important element of any movie. You can make a bad movie from a great script, but you can't make a good movie from a bad script (though many try).

T is for Talent.

U is for Underground Cinema, The name given to the cutting edge of cinema where filmmakers push the boundaries of filmmaking, and test the borders of cultural tolerance with the topics and storytelling techniques used. Many of the so-called "hip" filmmaking techniques employed by Hollywood are derived from Underground Cinema. Legendary experimental alternative filmmakers include Lech Kowalski, Jonas Mekas, Kenneth Anger, Don Letts, and Captain Zip.

V is for video and DVD duplication, the golden goose for independent filmmakers. Now that films are inexpensive and easy to reproduce, filmmakers can self-distribute their movies directly to the consumer, bypassing wholesalers and retailers.

W is for World Wide Web. Film may well become as available on the Internet as music in the future. These days, studios are deeply concerned about the possibility of a film equivalent to Napster.

Whip pan, when the camera pans quickly across a scene; a technique used by Quentin Tarantino.

X is for X-rated. The ratings or certificates awarded by the MPAA or the BBFC will greatly affect the sales potential of a film.

Y is for youth. The youth market (under 25) accounts for more than 70 percent of theater attendees.

Z is for Zombie, the film genre that seems to have launched every writer's, director's, or filmmaker's career in the United States. To mention just a few: *Reservoir Dogs*, *Return of the Secaucus Seven*, and *Night of the Living Dead*.

Lightweight dolly and track designed for use with video cameras.

Index

Page numbers in *italics*
refer to illustrations

Acknowledgements

A project such as this is never completed single-handedly. In my work at the Raindance Film Festival in London, I am lucky enough to meet incredibly talented people from all walks of life.

Thanks are due to those who have helped me write and illustrate this book: Kate Kirby, who originally pitched me the project, Dan Paolantonio and his film students at the Plymouth College of Art, and my producer, Xavier Rashid.

The staff at Raindance have supported me throughout the writing process: I am greatly indebted to Joe Pearshouse, Amelie Thille, Rory O'Donnell, and Dominic Thackray.

I owe especial thanks to the many interns who have passed through Raindance. Raindance, like so much of the film industry, is effectively run by interns.

Finally, I am deeply grateful to my wife and partner, Suzanne Ballantyne, without whose support I could never have completed this book.

Lastly, I thank all the talented writers, producers, directors, and filmmakers who have crossed my path. I thank you for the wisdom, shared experiences, and support that have enriched my life and made this book what it is.

Elliot Grove

Credits

Quarto would like to thank the following agencies and individuals for kindly supplying images for inclusion in this book:

- **Kobal:** p.12, 13, 16, 20, 24, 34, 35t, 36t/m, 61, 62, 64, 65, 73, 85, 92, 95
- **Allstar:** p.35b, 36b, 51, 74
- **Bridgeman:** p.45t/b
- **istockphoto**
- **Shutterstock**
- **RED Digital Cinema** www.red.com
- **p.15 Syd Field,** Paradigm www.sydfield.com
- **p.106 Broken Film** © Vicky Psarias, photography Vanessa Scott Thompson
- **Projector Films,** Tim Clague
- **Colin Taylor:** p.28

We would also like to thank Kevin Lindeman, Dan Martin, Grace Sergeant, and Chris Patmore for supplying images.

All other images are the copyright of Quarto Publishing plc. While every effort has been made to credit contributors, Quarto would like to apologize should there have been any omissions or errors, and would be pleased to make the appropriate correction for future editions of the book.

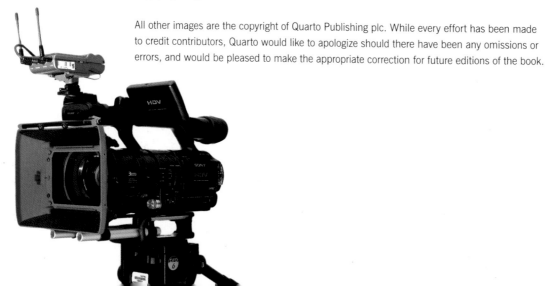